MEDIA DISQUISITIONS

Contemporary Media Discourses of 21st century

Dr Kriti Singh

KNOWLEDGE WORLD
KW Publishers Pvt Ltd
New Delhi

ISBN 978-93-89137-62-0 Paperback
eISBN 978-93-89137-63-7 ebook

Published in India by Kalpana Shukla

KNOWLEDGE WORLD

KW Publishers Pvt Ltd
4676/21, First Floor, Ansari Road
Daryaganj, New Delhi 110002
Phone: +91 11 23263498/43528107
Marketing: kw@kwpub.com
Editorial: production@kwpub.com
Website: www.kwpub.com

Printed and Bound in India

MEDIA DISQUISITIONS

Contemporary Media
Discourses of 21st century

I dedicate this book to all fallen soldiers who laid down their lives for the Tricolor, to the living veterans who dedicated their precious moments in the service of the nation, to all brave men and women who are defending my country, and to their families.

This book is also dedicated in memory of three beautiful souls who touched my life, my eldest brother Late Capt Ayush Attri (2003), my eldest son 'Bebu' (2009) & my Late Sister-in-Law Vandana Rathi (2016)

Contents

Foreword

The 'new media' are gradually, almost imperceptibly, aiding the rise of a Cyber Caliphate and governments and intelligence agencies are struggling to counter the enormous threat that it could pose in future. This threat will have wider ramifications than that manifested by the present Islamic Caliphate that controls a limited amount of territory. The unbridled expansion of the Cyber Caliphate and the long reach of its powerful tentacles are being fuelled by the power conferred by social media on non-state actors – organisations and individuals – who have nefarious designs on established governments and wish to re-shape the existing order to suit their thinking and their politics.

An individual in possession of a laptop with an Internet connection and owing allegiance to the so-called Caliph or Khalifa, whether in Bengaluru, or London, or New York or Paris, can actively propagate the thoughts of the Islamic State and seek recruits for the ISIS militia by exploiting the vulnerabilities of social media. A skilled hacker can intimidate leaders as well as ordinary citizens and manipulate social media to project the power of the Islamic State.

Social media

The cyber-warriors of the Islamic State are doing nothing more than exploiting the power and the reach of the new media. While traditional mass media – print, radio, television – still wield immense influence over mind-space, the new media – online newspapers, blogs, social media – whose content is available on-demand through the Internet and is accessible on any digital device, are gradually gaining prominence. Social media are changing the manner in which news is reported. The Hudson River plane landing (2009), the Virginia earthquake (2011), the US Special Forces raid on Osama bin Laden and several recent news items featuring celebrities were first reported on Twitter and were then picked up by the mainstream media.

In her book on contemporary media discourses, Prof. Kriti Singh provides an insightful commentary on the challenges facing the media. She examines the emerging role of new media, including social media like Twitter, Facebook and You Tube, among others, their power to reach large sections of the population quickly, and analyses their positive as well as adverse repercussions. She highlights the capacity of new media to create disaffection, and propagate radicalism – a tool for digital terrorism. She takes stock of the transformation in the gathering and the dissemination of news, the phenomenon of 'paid' news and all its ugly facets, and suggests measures to improve news journalism. India has a young population with a rapidly increasing number of impressionable netizens with access to new media. It is crucial that adequate stress is laid on the need for better regulation while simultaneously ensuring that legitimate users continue to enjoy free access.

The author analyses military-media relations and points out that, with skillful planning, the media can act as force multipliers. She justifies restrictions being imposed on serving defence personnel on joining social media as these can be used for gathering intelligence as well as undermining morale. However, she recommends using social media during humanitarian crises and disaster relief operations as a tool to reach out to the people affected the most by natural calamities. Recent floods in Jammu and Kashmir and Tamil Nadu provided evidence of such use.

Prof. Kriti Singh's book is meticulously researched and lucidly written. It offers a balanced perspective on contemporary media discourses and is an excellent addition to the scarce literature on this important subject. It provides readers – students, research scholars, academicians, media professionals, defence personnel – useful resource material about multifarious advancements in media studies.

My compliments to the author for this commendable effort. I am sure she will go on to build further on this research and earn more laurels in future. This book must be read by policy makers, the media community and analysts dealing with national security.

Brig Gurmeet Kanwal (Retd)
Former Director, Centre for Land Warfare Studies (CLAWS), New Delhi
Former Distinguished Fellow, Manohar Parrikar Institute for Defence Studies and Analyses (MP-IDSA), New Delhi
Adjunct Fellow, Wadhwani Chair in US-India Policy Studies, Center for Strategic and International Studies (CSIS), Washington, D.C.

Preface

Media has always been an embedded part of our social system. The simplistic drawings of ancient civilisation survival on caves to the sophisticated digital paintings created by powerful pro machines, flickering as holograms on the white surfaces depicting the complex life of 21st century metrosexual human, is also part of media. The urge to communicate and the dire need to survive have given humans communication power to create different vehicles of communiqué with his surroundings. The never-ending journey which continues at infinite level, begins from the womb to the continuous stages of communication, as today even the memories of deceased are also brought to life through the power of digital media.

The evolution of human communication and its intricate relationship with media has been a topic of interest for academicians, research and public discourses. The discourses which form intra, to interpersonal, to group, to public have always found media an intriguing subject, due to its versatile, dynamic nature, its dire need, its metamorphosis due to technology and the opportunities and challenges which it brings along. This book is an attempt to capture a few of the infinite narratives, click, tweets, frames that are constructed, shared, created and disseminated by media. It is a collection of essays written in the due span of time to understand, experience and narrate a few observations, information and knowledge, which was acquired by the me as a researcher while exploring growing possibilities in media, with special reference to the national security.

It constitutes different chapters, which endeavour to shed light on various aspects of media and its related dimensions. The beauty of media studies is that it can't be appreciated in the close structures of thinking, or in a defined curriculum. It is something, which is akin to brimming water making it ways in all directions. It is a labyrinth, layered and an extension of the complex human mind. An extension, which has human creativity at one side of the spectrum and artificial intelligence on the other side. The only way to understand and appreciate this phenomenon is to understand that there is a way through this maze, which helps humankind to create a common understanding despite infinite differences. The book will provide an opportunity for its readers to get a glimpse of the intricate world of media and its various dimensions.

Happy Reading!

Dr **Kriti Singh**
Assistant Professor
School of Communication
GD Goenka Univerisity
Sohna Haryana
&
Non-Resident Associate Fellow
Centre for Air Power Studies
Arjun Path, Subroto Park, New Delhi

Acknowledgements

I am wholeheartedly grateful for the tireless support and encouragement by my mentors and friends who have motivated me to work towards completion of this project. My late mentor Air Commodore Jasjit Singh AVSM, VrC, VM, who gave me the place at the Centre for Air Power Studies and the freedom to work on the topic of my choice. The continuous encouragement bestowed upon me by Air Marshal Vinod Patney SYSM PVSM AVSM VrC (Retd) (Ex Director General CAPS), Air Marshal KK Nohwar PVSM VM (Retd), Director General, CAPS, Air Vice Marshal Manmohan Bahadur VM (Retd), Additional Director General, CAPS. Dr. Manpreet Sethi and Dr. Shalini Chawla, the two iconic ladies who have always inspired me and tirelessly helped me in improving my writings.

Dr Juhi P Pathak, who invigorated me the importance of this project and encouraged me to finish what I started. I am also grateful to Mr. JP Dange (IAS) Former Chief Secretary, Government of Maharashtra, and Mr. Rajinder Kumar Kashyap, Joint Secretary, Ministry of Law and Justice for sharing their views and best wishes for my project. I am also grateful to Brig Gurmeet Kanwal (Retd.) for penning down encouraging words for the book. My special thanks to Mr. Pawan Agrawal, CEO Ocean Media and Defence and Security Alert, Mrs Mamata Jain, Director at Indian Council of Food and Agriculture and Dr. Sanjay Chillar for their support and encouragement. Last but not the least, I am grateful to my family, especially my father Mr. HL Attri for his continuous support and unconditional love. I am grateful to my spouse Capt. Manish Singh (Retd.). I am thankful to my son Manaansh Singh for giving me unconditional love and bearing with my work schedule. I am thankful to my elder brother like figure Wg Cdr Jaideep Mandodey, to my friends, including Ms Binu David, Wg Cdr Gajendra Tyagi, Dr. Stuti Banerjee, Dr. Sonali Huria and Mrs. Jyoti Bhatia, who have been a constant source of encouragement and motivation to me.

About the Author

Dr **Kriti Singh** is an Assistant Professor at the School of Communication (SoC), GD Goenka University (GDGU), Sohna, Haryana and a Non-Resident Associate Fellow at the Centre for Air Power Studies (CAPS), New Delhi. Her PhD thesis is on 'Indian Media-Military Relationship In Kashmir Conflict Post Kargil War: A Grounded Theory Study.' She has more than a decade work experience in media industry, research and academics. Her areas of interest are media-military relationship, media in conflict, media research, communication theories, qualitative research and cyber journalism.

An Alumni of Miranda House, Delhi University, she is Bachelor in English (Hons.), Master in Mass Communication and Journalism, E-MBA in Media Management, pursuing MA in International Relations, UGC–NET Qualified in Mass Communication and Journalism, PG. Diploma in Educational Administration and Supervision and PG. Diploma in Instructional Technology. She has also done various faculty development program (FDP), including FDP in 'Research and Pedagogy' from prestigious Indian Institute of Management, Ahmedabad. She is well versed with software program designed for computer assisted qualitative and mixed methods and the third Indian to be selected as MAXQDA Professional Trainer (VERBI Software, Germany).

She has done various online certifications from institutions of repute. To mention a few, she has done media and conflict related online certification like, 'Global Media, War, and Technology' from the University of Queensland, Certification in Conflict series from United Nations Institute for Training and Research (UNITAR), 'Conflict Analysis' and 'Interfaith Conflict Resolution' from US Institute of Peace (USIP). In terrorism studies, she has done her certifications in 'Terrorism and Counterterrorism: Comparing Theory and Practice' from Leiden University, 'New Approaches to Countering Terror: Countering Violent Extremism' from University of Maryland and 'Terrorism and Counterterrorism' from Georgetown. In research she has done her certifications in Qualitative Research Methods: Conversational Interviewing from Massachusetts Institute of Technology, 'Qualitative Research Methods' from University of Amsterdam and Qualitative Comparative Analysis (QCA) from Erasmus University Rotterdam. She is also Certified Web Analytics Professional, Business Communication Specialist and Certified Social Media Marketing Master from VSkills, a Joint Venture of Govt of India and Govt of Delhi.

Previously, she have been associated as an Assistant Professor, Dept. of Communication Studies, at Guru Gobind Singh Indraprastha University (GGSIPU) affiliated college, Jagannath International Management School (JIMS), Vasant Kunj, New Delhi, Assistant Professor at School of Media Studies, Jaipur National University, Jaipur, Associate Fellow and Media Coordinator for CAPS, Visiting Faculty, Media Centre, Young Women's Christian Association, Institute of Peace and Conflict Studies (IPCS), Times Internet and Doordarshan News.

She has nearing 80 publications under her name, including national and international journal, chapters in books, magazines and online publications. She has presented papers at seminar/conferences/roundtables at various national and international conference and seminar, including, University of Delhi, Sun Yat-sen University, Guangzhou, China, GD Goenka University, NASSCOM–DSCI Annual Information Security Summit, IAF Squadron Officer's Capsule Course, South Western Air Command, Kurukshetra University, Guru Gobind Singh Indraprastha University (GGSIPU), Commission For Scientific & Technical Terminology, Department of Higher Education, Ministry of Human Resource Development (MHRD), SCUBE Scientific Software Solutions, Wolfram Research Inc. Nepal Institute for International Cooperation and Engagement (NIICE) , Global Counter-Terrorism Council (GCTC) etc.

She is also affiliated to International Association for Media and Communication Research (IAMCR), IIQM Member Scholar Faculty, International Institute for Qualitative Methodology (IIQM), University of Alberta, Lifetime member for Centre for Education Growth and Research (CEGR) and Annual Member for Centre for Joint Warfare Studies (CENJOWS). She is also a key member for Capt Ayush Purusartha Foundation, a voluntary charitable organisation in memory of her late brother Capt Ayush Attri (18-03-1979 to 21-04-2003), New Delhi.

Introduction

Air Marshal KK Nohwar

From earliest times it was well understood that 'Knowledge is Power'. Indian Princes were always sent to gain knowledge from a learned teacher who was referred to as the Guru. His knowledge – obtained after a lifetime of study of the Vedas – was what gave him the ability to mould the young Princes into worthy leaders and just, unprejudiced and impartial kings, besides teaching them the martial arts.

The greatest of all Indian rulers, Emperor Ashoka (268-232 BCE), was deeply affected when he witnessed the carnage after winning the Kalinga War. He promised to renounce war and practice Ahimsa in future. But how would he let his subjects know of his intentions?

He got his edicts carved onto pillars of stone that were 40 to 50 feet high and set these up all around the peripheries of the Mauryan Empire. Remains of a large number of such pillars can still be found in the areas where his empire had spread – Afghanistan, Pakistan (of course, as that was part of India at the time), Nepal, entire India (except the Southern regions) till the Myanmar borders.

This was 'messaging' in all its glory; although it took several years for the message to be delivered – a far cry from the instant messaging that we have so grown used to in present times!

Today, thanks to the internet, one can communicate through the 'short message service' (commonly known as 'sms') across the globe in virtually the blink of an eye. Man's forays into space have, of course, made a significant difference to enable instant communication to every remote corner of the world.

Messaging was extremely important for rulers, particularly during the various campaigns that were being fought by them. Distances being large and automation having yet to be invented, ingenious methods were adopted to ensure that 'despatches' from the battlefield were sent to the ruler regularly for effective and timely intervention (sending reinforcements, etc.). Homing pigeons, despatch riders on horseback were some means utilised even in the medieval times, right till the invention of the telegraph. Red Indians in Northern America used smoke signals to convey messages over large distances, albeit within line-of-sight.

With the invention of the printing press in the mid fifteenth century, the stage was set for the spread of ideas to a larger cross-section of society. However, newspapers took almost another 150 years to appear on the scene.

The first newspaper made its appearance in 1605; this ensured wider outreach to common citizens across nations, initially in Europe, and slowly across the world.

The age of the print media had begun.

What was needed to convey thoughts and views across the world with greater conviction was visual media. This was achieved with the invention of photography in 1826 by Joseph Nicéphore Niépce of France (whose "View from the Window at Le Gras" became the first permanent photograph in the world), and Louis Daguerre, who, in 1839 in France, invented the first commercial photographic material (known as the Daguerreotype) and which really made photography a practical reality. The stage was now set for print media, assisted by visual media (in the form of still pictures initially), to really start shaping narratives among vast sections of society, most of whom were steeped in the 'seeing is believing' school of thought. These were early times, unaffected by 'photo-shopping', and media was a synonym for ethical reporting.

Photography progressed to film making as early as 1895. The ability to capture events in real time became the standard for War reporting which assumed importance during the two World Wars. Of course, the war correspondents often risked life and limb to report news from the battlefront.

The Vietnam War became the first War that was brought live directly into the bedrooms of the American people.

With the introduction of 24x7 reporting by Cable News Network (CNN), news could be seen by anyone across the world at any time. It was soon realised that mainstream media could have an impact on foreign policy formulations; this came to be known as the CNN Effect. During the 1991 Gulf War, news coverage was beamed live from targeted areas in Iraq where TV crew had been stationed. The report by CNN War correspondents of a Tomahawk cruise missile flying past their hotel bedroom window en route to its target a few blocks away was an unforgettable event of live news reporting, although it also showcased the chilling reality of the personal dangers faced by war correspondents reporting from the war zone.

In the early nineties fierce fighting broke out in Somalia between two warring clans that led to a civil war. By 1992 almost 4,00,000 Somalis died of disease, starvation, or as a direct result of the civil war. The war lords prevented UN food assistance from reaching the various relief camps set up by the UN. Therefore, in 1992, once the UNSC cleared a military mission (Op Restore Hope), the US President, George HW Bush, sent a contingent of US soldiers to Somalia to ensure that food assistance reaches the starving civilians. However, when the US Marines, in full war paint, landed at the Somali beach near the capital city of Mogadishu just before dawn on December 9, 1992, expecting to meet resistance from Somali gunmen, they were surprised when, instead, their landing was met with bright flashlights of TV crew 'awaiting' their arrival. This was a landmark event that was subsequently associated with the 'CNN Effect'.

In India, during the Kargil War – often referred to as India's CNN moment when the proceedings of the war were telecast live into bedrooms of Indian citizens – the involvement of the media to mould national and international opinion was 'by and large satisfactory' as acknowledged in the Kargil Review Committee's Report. Media was seen as a force multiplier and a tool of perception management by the military establishment after the Kargil War.

The paradigm had clearly shifted from 'Knowledge is Power' to 'Information is Power'.

That 'Information is (indeed) power' was to be proven just a couple of years later when the al Qaeda, making extensive use of the internet to gain information on flight timings, flight schools, make hotel bookings, obtain fake driver's licenses, etc., coordinated their activities on the world wide web using prearranged code words to carry out the 9/11 attacks.

Rapid strides in communication technology and gradual increase in social media platforms like Internet, Facebook, YouTube, and apps like Twitter, Instagram, Telegram, WhatsApp, etc. soon began to invade the privacy of individuals. These were exploited to create mass uprisings like the colour revolutions, Arab Spring, etc. before their use took a sinister turn. The rise of ISIS can be attributed to an aggressive campaign through social media for recruiting people across the world into the ranks of the ISIS. Using a combination of grisly videos of beheadings (of 'non-believers') that were posted on YouTube, the ISIS reached out to 'followers' and potential recruits through Twitter and Internet radio. Through use of social media their ranks swelled, beginning in 2014, enough for their leader to declare creation of a Caliphate; he claimed to have the required tools for the same, viz. religious legitimacy, effective governance and military prowess.

The rise of the ISIS went largely unchallenged in the initial days, till terrorist attacks around the world began to be claimed by ISIS followers. Only a concerted effort by some of the most powerful militaries of the world (the US, UK, Russia and France) ultimately saw the destruction of the Caliphate and the elimination of its leader – Abu Bakr al Baghdadi – in a Special Forces' operation (by the US' Delta Force) in North West Syria on October 26, 2019. Since the ISIS ideology was spread worldwide through the extensive use of social media, killing of its leader might not have had the desired impact on the activities of the ISIS, as its capabilities – for generating revenue – have remained unaffected, as has its command and control structure which has also remained untouched.

That social media and 'Fake News' could be used 'intelligently' to subvert the minds of the so-called intelligentsia across the Atlantic was unthinkable till the Presidential elections in the US began to gather steam in 2016. Time magazine in April 2019 has covered how the Russians went 'all out' to interfere with the 2016 US Presidential election, specially targeting the Hilary Clinton campaign by hacking into its website and also how they 'released politically damaging information on the internet; spread propaganda on Twitter, Facebook, YouTube and Instagram'.

When two former Cold War super-powers and arch rivals – that are today also military rivals – are on centre-stage for such 'damning' news, other nations just cannot draw comfort from such events. Such 'irresponsible' action tends to send a signal to other nations to echo exactly what the Editor mentions in the book 'Unrestricted Warfare' (written by two PLA Colonels) that "the first rule of unrestricted warfare is that there are no rules, with nothing forbidden." In the final analysis, some authors argue, it is very likely that the Russians did sway the outcome of the 2016 US Presidential elections.

Media reporting is getting even more complex with the introduction of AI and the use of drones. Today, reporters can use these 'faithful' tools to cover inaccessible terrain (damaged roads due floods, forest fires, earthquakes, landslides, volcanic eruptions, etc.) and get pictures of remarkable quality. These can rapidly be uploaded on social media and can reach an audience worldwide that stands at 4.54 billion reported internet users globally, representing 59 per cent of the world's population, as of January 2020. Those on other social media platforms like Facebook, Twitter, Instagram, WhatsApp, Snapchat, etc. would further share such information on their personal accounts with their respective groups, thereby achieving a multiplier effect. Perceptions and narrative creation, therefore, becomes easier today than it was anytime in the past. We saw a glimpse of how narratives can attempt to spin a web of lies to project that a successful strike by the IAF (at Balakot) on February 26, 2019 did not achieve anything at all, besides killing a crow! Yet, the Pakistani military 'opened' the facility (that had been struck by the IAF) to foreign and national (Pakistani) media only 43 days later! We will recall that very recently the Chinese had claimed that they had built a makeshift medical facility to treat up to 1,000 patients in barely ten days; so 're-doing' a damaged facility in 43 days is highly 'do-able' by a less-experienced nation than the Chinese.

In this game of winning the war of narratives, the media would continue to play an important part.

In her book, *Media Disquisitions*, Dr Kriti Singh very clearly brings out the ability of social media to reach large target audiences across the globe, its ability to create narratives that may be inimical to national security and, therefore, the need for nation states to guard against the ill effects of social media.

The book is well researched and makes for very interesting reading; it is as useful to the lay reader as it is for those in the armed forces, media, as well as those in government who would benefit from the various examples Professor Kriti has used to explain her point of view throughout the book.

I wish her greater success in her future writings.

1

Virtual Reality Journalism:

Changing the Narratives of News

The components of innovation and technology have always played a crucial role in progression of journalism, especially newsgathering aspect of reportage and news dissemination. In the past, where the newsgathering and dissemination techniques were based on writing, typing, telegraphy, telephone, wireless, the recent past witnessed a colossal transformation in it with the emergence of the Internet. Now, news can be gathered with the comfort of the Internet, transmitted digitally in binary codes and reach the masses spread across the globe, compressing time and distance barriers. Today, even social media updates like a 'tweet' can become an important and swift source of newsgathering and dissemination. Lately, we also saw the emergence of drone journalism, where the unmanned aerial vehicles are being used to gather news, especially from dangerous zones like wars and natural calamities, etc.

More recently the integration of virtual reality and 3-D (three-dimensional) environments in journalism has opened a new domain in journalism. The term virtual-reality (VR) was first coined by Jaron Lanier in 1987, the era, which witnessed an intense research endeavor happening in the field of VR.[1] However, the roots of VR can be traced back to the 19th century in the form of panoramic paintings of battles, etc. In modern times the emergence of smart phones, high-density displays, increased digitalisation, improved 3-D technology have provided breeding grounds for VR to flourish. Its impact can be felt in various facades of life and journalism is no exception. The VR technology gives the viewer an impression that they are actually on ground zero, witnessing the real event as it is unfolding, thus bringing them up close and personal to the real event, a process that will create great impression in their minds and hearts of the viewers.

Lately, news organisations are turning towards VR and 3-D technology to provide their viewers not only with sound and images but also 'feel' of news. In October 2015, the *New York Times* (NYT), in collaboration with Google, announced that they would distribute free virtual reality headsets to its readers. With these VR sets, the readers can watch VR films made by the NYT. The Google Cardboard device (Figs 1 and 2) is simply a piece of cardboard that turns any smartphone into a virtual reality headset, and which will provide its reader with 360-degree video, or what some call "immersive" video.[2] This was followed by Associated Press' (AP) plunge into VR as a journalism tool in partnership with RYOT, a Los Angeles-based production company.[3] One common feature in the use of VR by NYT and AP is that both the news organisations have shifted to the use of VR and 3D environments to roll out news based on refugees'/immigrants' plight and present 360 degree panoramic view to the audiences so that they can 'feel' the news, thus marking a paradigm shift in the news narration part of the news reporting. Both the news organisations are using short film based on news items transmitted via VR technology thus reinventing 'immersion journalism'.

Fig 1[4] **Fig 2[5]**

Google Cardboard Device

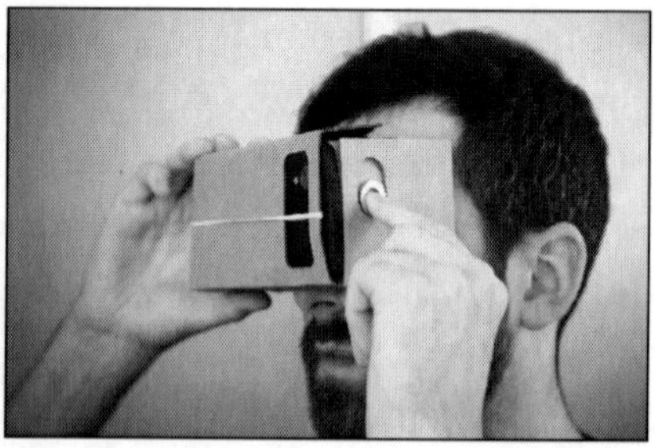

Immersion Journalism's methodology is to engage the reader's emotion and imagination using literary techniques to convey a story whose focus is on the experience, not the writer. The purpose of any immersion journalist is to determine the essence of "what it feels like," not "what occurred"[6]. And in this process the VR technology helps in creating the similar life like environment before the readers.

Another common feature about both these endeavours is that they both have tried to bring the horrors of displaced people to the viewers. Where the NYT VR project film about children uprooted by war[7] is "The Displaced,", the AP first film is 'Seeking Home: Life Inside the Calais Migrant Camp', a story about the largest migrant camp in Northern France.[8]

As quoted by Dean Baquet, the executive editor of the New York Times Magazine, "*The Displaced*, created the first critical, serious piece of journalism using virtual reality, to shed light on one of the most dire humanitarian crises of our lifetime."[9] According to NYT magazine editor Jake Silverstein, "The power of VR is that it gives the viewer a unique sense of empathic connection to people and events.... It has huge potential, to help bring viewers news and stories from the most inaccessible places".[10]

It is expected that the VR technology is going to transform the way we watch movies, play games, communicate, educate and a major change is expected in the field of journalism, both from newsmakers and news consumers' perspective. The NYT and AP virtual reality projects are steps in that direction. Despite the new avenues that the virtual journalism is capable of opening, there are serious debates happening regarding the ethics of reporting and objectivity in news.

To conclude, virtual reality is another convergence of traditional journalistic proficiencies with technology that has started creating ripples in the field of journalism. These technologies not only brought with them the increasing elements of timeliness, accuracy, reach, feel but also somewhere have started questioning the very 'human element' of 'newsmakers ' or 'news consumers.' The integration of VR technology in journalism has started to blur the boundaries between the reality and virtual reality, real experience and the virtual experience. The situation will get more challenging with the emergence of 'virtual-reality journalism broadcast' and its impact on various reporting, especially the war reporting.

The article was originally published on the Centre for Air Power Studies (CAPS) website.

2

Drone Journalism: Potential and Challenges

Man must rise above the Earth – to the top of the atmosphere and beyond – for only thus will he fully understand the world in which he lives.

– *Socrates*

Employment of aviation platforms in news journalism to gather news is not a new concept. The world of journalism witnessed the maiden use of aviation platforms with the use of the hot air balloon back in 1858, when multidimensional French photographer, balloonist and journalist Gaspard-Félix Tournachon (Nadar) took the first aerial photographs from the hot air balloon. This was followed by the use of fixed wing aircraft in the succeeding century and subsequently the emergence of Electronic News Gathering (ENG) through helicopters in the late 1970s.

Glancing through the modern history of journalism one can see how aviation technology and journalism have converged and mutually benefitted each other. Using aviation platforms to collect news stories was actually a turning point in journalism as it was breaking away from the traditional news gathering means. But the crucial question that arises is 'What was the need to employ them?' Some possible reasons: the colossal expansions of news channels, the 24x7 news transmission capabilities, cut-throat competition between the news channels, the unending consumption of news stories and increasing resourcefulness of news media houses.

And today, journalism is eyeing another aviation platform, whose use would not only pose challenges but if used judiciously, could open new avenues for newsgathering process in journalism. Indeed, the use of Drones or Remotely Piloted Aircraft Systems (RPAS) is all set to revolutionize the electronic newsgathering.

Since their origin in World War I, drone technology has unlocked abundant opportunities in both the defence and civil sectors. In military use we have seen the employment of Drones as Predators or Reapers that have been continuously used against adversaries in targeted 'hot' battlefields. But in the military sector the use of Drone is stained with blood and controversies both, especially the use of drones by the US in Afghanistan and Pakistan, which had caused a lot of hue and cry. For instance, American CIA drones had targetted Pakistan more times in US President Obama's first year in office than in the previous five years combined.[11] However, we have also seen the successful use of Drones in the war against terrorism. These strikes have, since 9/11, killed more than half of the 20 most wanted Al Qaeda suspects, the Uzbek, Yemeni and Pakistani heads of allied groups and hundreds of militants.[12]

This brings us to the next question: 'Is the use of drones in journalism a wise move?' According to the report released by the Bureau of Investigative Journalism report, (a UK-based non-profit) in the last five years, the Obama administration has launched more than 390 drone strikes. Averaging 78 strikes per year, the death toll in that time frame is up to 2,400. In Pakistan alone, between 416 and 951 civilians, including 168 to 200 children, have been killed.[13] The same fear is resonant by Human rights watch. Given the quantum of damage and bloodshed drones have already incurred in military use, its employment in journalism cannot be that appealing.

Meanwhile, in journalism, the use of RPAS is presenting itself as an exciting opportunity. Talking about the technological, policymaking and journalism potential of the RPAS, the advantages are many, as identified below:

- Since the RPAS are much cheaper as compared to helicopters, their use presents itself as a more lucrative technology in the backdrop of tight budgets, which the media houses face.
- Drones can be an advanced tool for extensive news gathering and with lower operational costs, news gathered aerially can get space in various news media channels, print, online and broadcasting medium.

- As the RPAS doesn't require any human element within the machine itself, it can make a reporter's job easier and less dangerous. RPAS have the ability to reach places where it is physically not possible for reporter to reach, such as a fire incident, police firing, terror strike, disaster news, etc.
- As drones come in different shapes and sizes, the journalist can customise them as per their requirements, thus providing flexibility in terms of technology to the journalist.

However, the use of this technology will have its own set of challenges as described below:

- The use of drones would require news organisations to redesign their existing policies. As of now, the use of choppers and other aircraft comes with a contract. But with RPAS one would not require any contract, so at the organisational level, policies, rules will have to be set keeping in mind the possibilities of abuse (e.g. infringement of privacy, entering prohibited/restricted areas, etc.).
- Complexities of operating varying drone models would require the availability of additional skilled human resource.
- The use of drones for Electronic News Gathering (ENG) could create difference of interest and generate complexities for the law enforcing agencies and media houses. As the former will try to limit their use and the latter will try to exploit RPAS to their advantage, in these situations a conflict of interest is likely to emerge.
- With more aviation vehicles hovering over cities, their management will pose a challenge to the air traffic management and law enforcement agencies, especially in terms of emergency services, which may be hampered by these flying objects.
- A mammoth task before the policy makers will emerge to synchronize the use of RPAS for newsgathering purpose within the existing legal framework.
- There would be challenges pertaining to the privacy issues. As these RPAS could be misused to trespass the privacy of people, we could see the emergence of air paparazzi.

- From journalism point of view, use of drones is a challenge as already journalism is criticised for invading the privacy of others in the name of freedom of expression. So, with this new technology in hand, at a time when we have already witnessed the sensationalisation of news, tabloid journalism, and how the journalist and media owners are going to chart out regulations will indeed be a tricky task. Journalism wants to work in an unbinding environment, whereas this technology needs to be regulated.

With the emergence of new technology, also comes the fear of its abuse and the use of drones in journalism will be no different. The same fear was resonant with the coming of computers that they will replace the human being one day, or when the Internet was introduced to the civilian sector from the military sector. Today, drones provide countless opportunities in defence, surveillance, farming, scientific experiments, disaster management, etc. For journalism in particular, the media houses have to first evaluate their needs and then create a sound system where this technology can be put to best use. It should be used to raise the standards of journalism to a new height, while performing with ethics so that the watchdog 'eye in the sky', does not breach the trust and safety of people for whom the news is being gathered.

The article was originally published on the Centre for Air Power Studies (CAPS) website.

3

Through the Lens of New Media

What's interesting about the shift from an industrial age to a technological age is that we keep inventing new media: movies, records, radio, television, the Internet, and now e-books – and one of the things that's most interesting about the invention of a new medium is watching it reinvent itself as it penetrates the culture.

– *David Gerrold*

To define new media with a single answer is an impossible task. Even old media were once new, and today's new media is also constantly changing and evolving.[14] New Media can broadly be understood to include the use of new communication technologies for old or new purpose, a new way of using old technologies, and, in principle, all other possibilities for the exchange of social meaning.[15] Historically, new media didn't happen in a flash but originated from the media prior to it. Our understanding of new media largely comes from looking into the "rear-view mirror," as Marshall McLuhan observed.[16]

'When faced with a totally new situation,' McLuhan famously says, 'we tend always to attach ourselves to the objects, to the flavor of the most recent past. We look at the present through a rear-view mirror. We march backwards into the future.'[17] As is the case with most of McLuhan's ingenious labels for profound relationships in media, once you begin looking for rear-view mirrorisms, you see them everywhere you turn in history. The telephone was first called the talking telegraph;

the automobile the horseless carriage; the radio the wireless.[18] Indeed, the rear-view becomes, for McLuhan, a fundamental operating principle for the evolution of media and its effect. Thus, new media, although the term refers to new, however, it is the traditional media which has reinvented itself with changing times and technologies.

Defining New Media

In simple terms 'new media' in general refers to those digital media that are interactive, incorporate two-way communication, and involve some form of computing as opposed to the 'old media' such as the telephone, radio and TV. These older media, which in their original incarnation did not require computer technology, now in the present configuration are making use of computer technology. As defined by the Oxford Dictionary, 'new media means of mass communication using digital technologies such as the Internet.' New Media is the form of communicating in the digital world, which includes publishing on CDs, DVDs and, most significantly, over the Internet.[19]

The boundaries between the traditional media and new media have blurred. New media technologies enabled the same content to flow through various channels and assume many different forms at the point of reception. Thus was initiated the process of media convergence.[20] The positive side of the new media technologies is that they have brought down the production and distribution costs, increased the delivery channels, enhanced the reach of the existing delivery channels, presented various options to the consumers, and provided the consumer the means to maintain archives, interpret, and share the media content in various channels, thereby creating greater impact. However, the flip side of these new media technologies is that they have augmented the concentration of ownership, especially in mainstream media, where only a group of 'elites' is dominating the media sector.

New Media Landscape in India

The recent decade saw the strong emergence of new media in India. At present the Indian new media landscape has got a boost with rapid technological innovations along with optimistic changing patterns and growth in the media industry. Today, Indian new media is buzzing with the technological developments like social media interactive platforms, podcasts, RSS feeds, micro blogs, websites, online instant messaging services, etc., which have transformed the very dynamics of the Indian media landscape. One can witness the amalgamation of the real world with virtual, traditional media with the digital and passive audience transforming into active audience. This new landscape has its own challenges and potentials and has initiated a new era in the Indian media industry based on three important factors, i.e., to connect, to collaborate and to create.

Indian new media at present

Following are the key highlights from the 2013 India Digital Future in Focus report[21] by comScore:[22]

- Indian online population currently ranks as the 3rd largest in the world after China and the US. Around 73.9 million home and work Internet users are in India.
- It surpassed Japan in March 2013 and registered a year-over-year (YoY) growth of 31 per cent.
- Seventy-five per cent of its Internet users are under the age of 35.
- India has the youngest skewing online population among Brazil, Russia, India and China (BRIC) countries.
- Across all age and gender groups, women between the ages of 35-44 years old are the heaviest Internet users in the Indian market.
- The Indian blogging audience grew 48 per cent in the past year to 36 million visitors, while 26 per cent of category traffic comes from mobile phones and tablets.
- Fifty-four million Internet users in India watched online videos on their computer, representing a 27 per cent increase over the past year.
- Predominantly, the Internet user uses mobiles to access the Internet and various social media platforms.
- About 17 per cent of the Indian population is between 15 and 24 years old, and they are experiencing the changes brought by new media

technologies most dramatically in their personal and professional lives.[23]

- The access of the new media technology by Indians, including young Indians, depends heavily on social locations – including gender, caste, class, and place of residence – in this highly stratified society,[24] thus creating a digital divide between those who have access to the new media technologies and those who don't.

Future Trends

The future trend indicates that the new technologies and innovations will continue to alter the dynamics of new media in terms of, content/message production, information dissemination and the audience participation. The changes will bring challenges before the authorities, especially when it comes to freedom of expression. In terms of freedom, we will also witness the 'attempts by traditional authorities to control the new media use of young people through discourses on sexual danger and moral panic.'[25] The recent ban on the documentary 'India's Daughter' by BBC is one such example. Furthermore, the Indian new media will continue to witness the strain between the commercial consumption of new media technologies by the country's growing middle class and the use of these same technologies for development purposes.[26] On the front of increasing digital divide challenge, in order to fill this chasm and to equip the large number of economically backward Indians who can potentially be served by new media technologies, commercialisation and Information and communication technologies for development (ICTD)[27] will continue to work together in so-called Bottom of the Pyramid (BoP) initiatives. Attempts to provide Indians with access to computers are a good example of such programmes.[28] More advanced media devices with better access to social media platforms will be also seen in coming times.

To conclude, from today's perspective, some apparently major challenges are posed by the impact of (now) new media technologies, like the ephemeral nature of online content and social media communication or the hybridisation and amalgamation of public and private spheres on the web; in other words, these are the challenges posed by digitalisation.[29]

And the Indian new media landscape will be no exception in terms of challenges but have a huge potential, which can be tapped to make Indian smart cities with knowledge based society.

The article was originally published on the Centre for Air Power Studies (CAPS) website.

4

Paid News:
A Curse on News Journalism

Because today we live in a society in which spurious realities are manufactured by the media, by governments, by big corporations, by religious groups, political groups ... So I ask, in my writing, What is real? Because unceasingly we are bombarded with pseudo-realities manufactured by very sophisticated people using very sophisticated electronic mechanisms.

– Philip K. Dick

The concept of "paid news" is not new to the media or society. The ailment has been quite long-standing, complicated and deep-seated in the prevailing structure. However, in the recent times the phenomenon of 'paid news' has acquired serious dimensions. Today it goes beyond the corruption of individual journalists and media companies and has become pervasive, structured and highly organised. In the process, it is undermining democracy in India. This has anguished the leading sections of the society, including political leaders, thinkers, journalists and media owners. [30]

Press Commission of India (PCI) defines paid news as, "Any news or analysis appearing in any media (Print & Electronic) for a price in cash or kind as consideration." As per the guidelines of the PCI on the paid news, it clearly states that, "news should be clearly demarcated from advertisements by printing disclaimers, should be strictly enforced by all publications. As far as news is concerned, it must always carry a credit line and should be set in a typeface that would distinguish it from advertisements."

In 2003, the *Times of India* initiated its 'Next Big Thing-Medianet' when Bennett, Coleman Company Limited (BCCL) redefined the 'definition of information' and initiated 'paid content service' or 'advertorials about products or services'. Medianet has been blamed for the opening of the Pandora's Box of paid news epidemic. Subsequently, in 2004, the Election Commissioner detected the menace of paid news during parliamentary elections. Later, in 2009, the presence of paid news was strongly felt during the general elections. In 2014, EC confirmed approximately 787 cases of paid news and around 3,100 notices were issued to the violators, including former chief ministers Madhu Koda and Ashok Chavan. Lately, during the Delhi Legislative Assembly Election-2015, around twenty cases of paid news were confirmed.

The key reasons identified behind paid news are: corporatisation of media, desegregation of ownership and editorial roles, decline in autonomy of editors/journalists due to emergence of contract system and poor wage levels of journalists, lack of political will to end this menace. In addition to this, there is media-politicians nexus. The press council acknowledged that a section of Indian media had 'indulged in monetary deals with some politicians and candidates by publishing their views as news items and bringing out negative news items against rival candidates' during the last elections. Another reason is that the existing regulatory bodies like News Broadcasting Standards Authority, Broadcasting Content Complaints Council, Press Council of India (PCI) and Electronic Media Monitoring Centre (EMMC), are not well organised and lack powers to deal with the paid news. Also there are blurred jurisdiction boundaries within these multiple organisations like ECI, PCI, Ministry of Information and Broadcasting (MoIB), etc., thus creating ambiguity in terms of jurisdiction. Furthermore, the prevailing provisions to penalise lawbreakers are also ineffective.

But what makes paid news a problem is, first, that paid news hoodwinks the public and obstructs their capability to form correct judgments and accurate opinions. The content of paid news is designed to achieve a certain effect or result by the parties who have invested their money in the development of content. Therefore, the content, be it news, opinion, or feature that is served to the readers, audience or leaders misleads the public. Second, continuous flow of paid news influences the voters' behaviors, thus damaging the electoral process. Third, it masquerades advertisements as news, as there is a deliberate attempt by the publisher to pass off an advertisement as news, thus again misleading the people. Fourth, it violates the election laws and spending norms. Fifth, it destroys the very soul of news journalism, which exists on the elements of truth, fairness, objectivity, accuracy, responsibility, impartiality, and fair play and exploits the freedom of the press.

The remedy for the paid news is responsibility of all sections of the media and society, as it is a threat to any democratic process. First, there is a need to frame an all-inclusive legal definition of 'paid news' in order to avoid the prevailing ambiguity in this regard. Second, a mechanism needs to be built to identify the paid news. Third, in order to maintain the autonomy of editors/journalists, an established organisation like MoIB needs to continuously or periodically check the prevailing status of editors/ journalists. Fourth, the financial stakes of the media houses, including editors and news producers, need to be scrutinised. Fifth, the media houses need to disclose the 'private treaties' undertaken by them with other organisations that are the source of advertising revenue generation for the media house. Sixth, increasing the power of PCI and, on similar lines, establishing a body for electronic media which can take strong action against the offenders, is the need of the hour. Last, at the grass root level, the emphasis should me more on ethical and objective reporting rather than the TRPs, and this is a collective endeavor where audience shun the unethical reporting and media houses stop serving the audience irresponsible, unethical paid news.

The article was originally published on the Centre for Air Power Studies (CAPS) website.

5

Social Media and the Web of Social Engineering

Our social tools are not an improvement to modern society, they are a challenge to it.

– Clay Shirky

Communication has evolved along with the evolution of mankind. In contemporary times, social media has emerged as another revolution within the infinite realms of communication in general and mass media in particular. Social media has altered the very way the human communicates and connects. It has surpassed the boundaries of time, nations, races, and cultures and brought diversities of the globe on one platform. Having said so, one cannot deny the flip side of this development of the information society whose information hunger refuses to die down. One of the core vulnerabilities of the social media is the threat of social engineering or manipulation and the lethality which it initiates in the digital world that can affect the real world.

Social Engineering: The existence of social engineering or social manipulation is as old as the history of communication, as it is a skill of influencing an individual's mind with the crafty skill of communication. It is a combination of science and creativity. The concept seeks to identify the vulnerability of the human element rather than the computer network.[31] Social engineering, as called by hackers, is the 'art' of utilising human behaviour to breach security without the participants (or victims) even realising that they have been manipulated.[32] Phishing, spam, baiting, spoofing or hacking, dumpster diving are some of the techniques used by social hackers.

Why Social Media is a Breeding Ground for Social Engineers?

With increasing digital penetration and multiple interactive digital platforms booming, the social media has become more and more integrated in our lives. To majority of Internet users social media is just one another activity; to many, an 'important activity' of a day. From personal communication to business communication, social media has acquired an absolute new meaning and multi dimensions. However, this integration of social media has also made it a breeding ground for the social engineers to flourish for the following reasons:

- **Fertile Ground for Intelligence Gathering:** Social media provides a fertile ground for a social engineer who is on the look-out for information. As more and more users circulate their personal information, location information, travel plans, photographs, job details, videos, the more fodder they provide to the social engineer and unknowingly assist him in making them more vulnerable targets.
- **Real Human Hackers with Fake Profiles:** Social media is another exposed ground where the social engineers are emerging as major threats. If we see social engineering from the lens of social media, we can redefine it as an activity where a hacker creates convincing fake profiles to connect and interact with a target or group of targets. Hackers create the profiles, build up a network of connections to make them appear trustworthy, and eventually connect with their actual target. Once the request is accepted a hacker can steal information or launch a cyber-attack. Instead of a promising HR, marketing, or sales lead, profiles can be a serious cyber security threat.[33]
- **Simplicity Increases Vulnerability:** The simplicity of the social media platforms in terms of uploading and sharing the content like photos, videos, blogging, messenger services has made it user friendly, thus more popular within the users. However, this simplicity also

comes with the flip side, as these users are the prime targets of the social engineers. While elaborating on the abuse of the social media platforms, the Symantec 2014 Internet Security Threat Report states, "Unfortunately, widespread popularity draws scammers to these social networking platforms, as per the saying, '*If you build it, they will come.*' If a social network attains a certain level of popularity, scammers will find a way to exploit it. In 2012 the shift in spam and phishing towards social media was already underway, although these threats were harder to recognise than their email counterparts. Symantec identified new scams targeting some of these up-and-coming social networks during 2013."

- **Freebies come with a Price:** For a social engineer, social media is one of the cheapest ways to first infiltrate in the virtual social structures, then create an account, foster relationship with the online users, as the majority of the social media platforms comes free of cost for the user. You just need to have an Internet, an email account and can easily access social media platforms like Facebook, LinkedIn, YouTube, and Twitter, etc. After winning the confidence of the set target, the social engineer can lure them into the virtual trap or real traps and accomplish the desired aim.
- **New Breeding Grounds for Phishing and Spam:** Social media has alternated the trend in phishing and spam. Where previously the social manipulators relied heavily on emails, today the trend is more towards using social media platforms to locate targets. Now, from a crafty email it has transformed into crafty social media campaigns designed by the social engineers to trap their targets. Although the style of phishing or spam has evolved, but the things or materials to lure the target remains the same. It can be free movie tickets, gift cards, electronic goods, bogus offers, etc.

To conclude, there is no denial of the fact that social media is growing and changing every moment, every day. So are the challenges, and social engineers or human hackers are one such challenge. Amongst multiple communication platforms, social media has carved a niche for itself.

Where it has emerged as a fertile ground for popularity and profit both, sadly it has also provided the breeding grounds for the social manipulators. The answer doesn't lie in shunning of this magnificent dimension of communication but the judicious use of social media and countermeasures to deal with social engineers.

The article was originally published on the Centre for Air Power Studies (CAPS) website.

6

Digital Terrorism: Choreographing the Terror

Approximately forty percent of the total world's population is connected with the internet in some way or the other. In the span of more than a decade since the beginning of the 21st century, it is estimated that the number of people connected to the internet has increased ten times. The mark of 1 billion internet users was crossed in 2005 and within five more years the number crossed the mark of 2 billion. And by the end of 2014 it crossed the mark of 3 billion users. According to the statistics provided by Internet Live Stats, in 2014, the highest internet users were from China, United States and India respectively. China registered 64,16,01,070 internet users with 4 per cent annual growth rate, followed by US with 27,98,34,232 internet users with 4 per cent annual growth rate. India registered 24,31,98,922 internet users with 14 per cent annual growth rate.[34] Around 19.19 per cent of the Indian population has access to the internet.

However, the internet is a dual use tool. On the one hand, it helps transform societies into smart information societies. On the other hand, it can also become a breeding ground for societal evils to flourish, to communicate, to collaborate, to manage perceptions and distort political discourses and manipulate public opinions across the globe.

With the boom of Internet users in the 21st century, one of the alarming trends is the emergence of 'digital terrorism.' As societies get more and more electronically connected, the more they become vulnerable to digital terrorism. The reach and impact of digital terrorism is also extensive. It ranges from spreading hatred and extremist propaganda through social networks to malicious defacing of websites to organised theft of sensitive information, to bringing down servers and networks.[35] Internet comprises of both information warfare and cyber terrorism. Digital terrorism presents frightening possibilities for crippling vital economic, social, governmental, and other infrastructure.[36]

Due to the advancement in the information and communication technologies and with the world turning into a 'global village,' the spaces between the world populations have started to blur. The negative sides of these advancements are that the terrorist networks can coordinate their activities from any corner of the world by using the same platforms, which can result in a coordinated attack on the 'target' with utmost precision. The 2011 Mumbai attacks is one such example where the terrorists were in continuous communication with their masters across the border. In the 2008 Mumbai attacks, the *Lashkar-e-Taiba* used Google Earth extensively to plan their attacks. Through the use of digital technologies, international terrorists have an unprecedented capability to obtain, process and protect information from law enforcement investigations. They can use the interactive capabilities of advanced computers and telecommunications systems to plot terrorist strategies against their 'targets' all over the globe, to find the most efficient routes and methods for financial transactions, and to create international virtual networks for counterintelligence purposes.[37]

With shrinking spaces, mushrooming of infinite common digital interactive platforms – where one can share the information or ideas across the globe in nano seconds – the digital terrorists are transforming the Internet into a lethal weapon. According to a study conducted by RAND on the use of the internet in terrorism and extremism, the Internet may enhance opportunities for 'potential recruits' to become radicalised. It may act as an 'echo chamber' for extremist beliefs; in other words, the internet may provide a greater opportunity than offline interactions to confirm existing beliefs. It appears to facilitate this process of radicalisation, and it increases opportunities for self-radicalisation.[38] The social media use by the Islamic State of Iraq and Syria (ISIS), the al-Qaida's shift in its propaganda apparatus from old video/audio cassettes to online platforms a decade back and the Taliban's use of the internet through websites are few examples.

One of the key efforts of the terrorist organisations is to produce the "shock and awe" effect on the masses. To achieve this aim, the digital platforms provide them the cheapest, easiest and fastest ground to choreograph their acts of terrorism. By doing so, the brutal acts of terror acts are glorified and spread on the digital platforms, like ISIS videos on social media, thus in a way accomplishing the terror group's desired objective. The use of digital platforms has emerged as a complex propaganda tool in the virtual world by the terrorist groups and has facilitated in shaping the perceptions of people both at home and outside. Underlying the effect of digital terrorism in Afghanistan, the International Crisis Group report revealed, "The result is weakening public support for nation-building, even though few actively support the Taliban."

These examples display that digital terrorism is here to stay and won't just confine itself to propaganda, but will also breed and pollinate new ideas and innovations. The deployment of sophisticated digital terrorism as a strategy has redefined the parameters of propaganda. The terrorists' aim can be nullified if a certain mechanism can be built to blackout these choreographed digital terrorist acts. A counter digital terrorism strategy is the need of the hour where the enemy propaganda can be countered with positive propaganda. In addition, we have to equip internet users to differentiate between the noises and voices on these platforms and to make them aware how an ordinary user can fall in the trap of digital terrorism. We have to make internet users understand the impact of 'share' and report abuse buttons since with one share button any user can indirectly become part of circulating the propaganda choreographed by terrorist networks.

The article was originally published on the Centre for Air Power Studies (CAPS) website.

7

Battle of Narratives:
Media as Soft Power an Indian Perspective

The destiny of the world is determined less by the battles that are lost and won than by the stories it loves and believes in.

– Harold Goddard

The Concept

Power is the ability to affect the behaviour of others to get the outcome you want, and there are three basic ways to do that:

- You can coerce them with threats.
- You can induce them with payments
- Or you can attract and co-opt them.

However, soft power rests on the ability to shape the preferences of others.[39] In a simple term, soft power is, "A persuasive approach to international relations, typically involving the use of economic or cultural influence."[40] The term 'soft power' was coined by US origin political scientist Joseph S. Nye Jr., back in 1990's in his book *Bound to Lead: The Changing Nature of American Power*. Soft power often allows a leader to save on costly carrots and sticks. The similar concepts had already been introduced in other disciplines such as Gramsci's hegemony, Bourdieu's symbolic power, Weber's authority, Foucault's disciplinary power, and Habermas' communicative power.[41] However, simply put, in behavioral terms, soft power is attractional power.[42] However, on the flip side, there is continued confusion in some sections of international relations whether soft power is the power of attraction or confusion?[43]

Figure 1: Behavioural Power

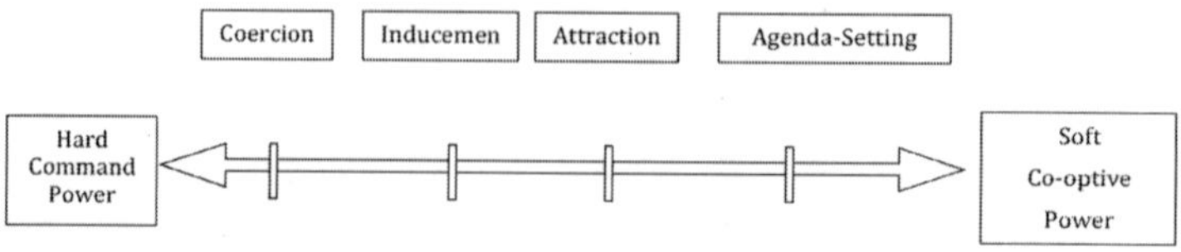

Source: J. Nye, *Bound to Lead*, p. 267.

Soft power can be roughly categorised into 5 categories in accordance with the policy goals to achieve. They are:[44]

- Soft power to improve external security environment by projecting peaceful and attractive images of a country;
- Soft power to mobilise other countries' supports for one's foreign and security policies;
- Soft power to manipulate other countries' way of thinking and preferences;
- Soft power to maintain unity of a community or community of countries;
- Soft power to increase approval ratings of a leader or domestic support of a government.

MEDIA AS SOFT POWER: A PANORAMIC VIEW

While highlighting the media's role as a soft power, Nachman Shai,[45] a former journalist who currently serves as a member of the Knesset, said, "The media has played a significant role in this shift from hard to soft power." Shai, while presenting an illustration to support his views on media as soft power, emphasised, "In the Palestine conflict, Israel used to enjoy a monopoly over the flow of information. But Palestine has learned to play the game." Further, he elaborated that Palestine has "developed communication perception … and created an alternative source of information from Israel's."[46] Speaking on similar lines, Dawood Azami from the BBC World Service (London) agreed that world power is shifting from one set of actors to another set of actors. In this shift, we will see a 'battle of narratives' being played out, as different stories are being told of the shifts in geopolitical power. The media's role will be instrumental in these power contests.[47]

A strong nation is an outcome of various powers merging into one and also to a large extent the projection of their strengths and powers in the international arena. A strong projection can to a great degree mould or change the perceptions and opinions of the people, within as well as outside the country. And for making a positive projection with a fruitful outcome depends largely on the nation branding in the eyes of the world, where the media can play a tremendous role. Besides, the media can play an extraordinary role in maintaining equilibrium, in the multi-culture, multi-religion and multi-civilisations existing across the globe. It can act as a bridge and connect various nations and communities with each other; a window which can provide a glance to a country's internal life, culture, traditions, irrespective of distance and distinctions.

INDIAN PERSPECTIVE

Historically, India has always been the centre of attraction and dissemination of rich culture, knowledge, values and traditions. India's strong cultural and knowledge influence echoes in the various historic civilisations like Mesopotamia, Rome Greece, etc. India has been a major exporter of human and intellectual capital to universities, transnational corporations, and multilateral organisations in the West. Today, as one of the fastest growing economies and a vibrant, pluralist, and secular polity, India is increasingly viewed as an economic and political power.[48] Although poorer and less economically dynamic than China, India has soft power in abundance. It is committed to democratic institutions, the rule of law and human rights. As a victim of jihadist violence, it is in the front rank of the fight against terrorism. It has a huge and talented diaspora. It may not want to be co-opted by the West but it shares many Western values. It is confident and culturally rich.[49] India thus offers unprecedented opportunities to study soft power in a globalised world with a media and communication infrastructure that enables the rapid global interchange of ideas and influences.[50]

A closer look at India's media power reveals that in contrast with the western countries trend, the Indian media industry is booming. According to the Federation of Indian Chambers of Commerce and Industry (FICCI) and KPMG 2013 report, "The Indian Media and Entertainment industry grew from INR 728 billion in 2011 to INR 820 billion in 2012, registering an overall growth of 12.6 percent."[51] The same trend has been witnessed in the current year. The latest report released in March 2014, titled 'Economic Contribution of the Indian Motion Picture and Television Industry', by leading financial services firm, Deloitte, points out, "The Indian motion picture and television industry is one of the largest and fastest growing

Table 1: Overall Industry Size and Projection[53]

Overall Industry Size (Rs billion) (for calendar years)	2007	2008	2009	2010	2011	2012	Growth in 2012 over 2011 (%)	2013P	2014P	2015P	2016P	2017P	CAGR (2012-2017) (%)
TV	211.0	241.0	257.0	297.0	329.0	370.1	12.5	419.9	501.4	607.4	725.0	847.6	18.0
Print	160.0	172.0	175.2	192.9	208.8	224.1	7.3	241.1	261.4	285.6	311.2	340.2	8.7
Films	92.7	104.4	89.3	83.3	92.9	112.4	21.0	122.4	138.3	153.6	171.7	193.3	11.5
Radio	7.4	8.4	8.3	10.0	11.5	12.7	10.4	14.0	15.4	18.7	22.7	27.4	16.6
Music	7.4	7.4	7.8	8.6	9.0	10.6	18.1	11.6	13.1	15.3	18.3	22.5	16.2
OOH	14.0	16.1	13.7	16.5	17.8	18.2	2.4	19.3	21.1	23.0	25.0	27.3	8.4
Animation and VFX	14.0	17.5	20.1	23.6	31.0	35.3	13.9	40.6	46.9	54.2	63.1	73.5	15.8
Gaming	4.0	7.0	8.0	10.0	13.0	15.3	17.7	20.1	23.8	30.9	36.2	42.1	22.4
Digital Advertising	4.0	6.0	8.0	10.0	15.4	21.7	40.9	28.3	37.1	48.9	65.1	87.2	32.1
Total	**514.5**	**579.8**	**587.4**	**651.9**	**728.4**	**820.5**	**12.6**	**917.4**	**1058.5**	**1237.5**	**1438.4**	**1661.1**	**15.2**

sectors, contributing US$ 8.1 billion (c. Rs 50,000 Cr.) to the country's economy, equating to 0.5 per cent of GDP, in 2013. The sector also supports a significant 1.8 million (18.8 lakh) jobs.[52] These facts and figures display the might of the Indian media industry.

To win the minds and hearts of people, media's soft power plays an extensive role. For example, the integral part of the media industry, Bollywood, plays a key role in winning the minds and hearts of people across the world. The Middle East is Bollywood's third-largest overseas market and growing so rapidly that many Bollywood movies now hold premieres in Dubai on opening night. Dubai is even erecting a Universal Studios-like Bollywood theme park. But the Muslim country, mostly in the grip of Bollywood mania is Pakistan, India's cultural twin in every respect but religion. As with the Beatles under communism, the more aggressively Pakistani authorities have tried to purge Bollywood from their soil, the more its popularity has grown.[54]

CONCLUSION

The present and the future of the countries of this 'global village' are tied together with economic and resource dependency, issues of global concern like environment, depleting resources, terrorism, etc. The intertwining of hard power and soft power is one of the answers to the global concerns. The media's role as soft power can't be denied. The global reach of Indian media is immense, but its huge potential is yet to be optimised. The Indian media industry is growing at an immense speed and according to analysts, by 2050, it will supersede USA also. To conclude, according to Professor Daya Thussu, University of Westminster, "India's Soft Power includes Buddhism and its influence over large swathes of people, "Bollywood" and its yet uncharted influence, the worldwide 'Yoga industry', and finally the very large and widely spread Indian diaspora." To conclude, with former Minister of State for External Affairs Shashi Tharoor words, "it is not the size of the army that wins but the country that tells the better story." And there is no better storyteller than media.

The article was originally published in the Defence and Security Alert Magazine.

8

New Media-Military Relationship: Overview and Challenges

New media includes all those platforms that empower a broad range of actors (individuals through nation-states) to create and disseminate near-real time or real time information with the ability to affect a broad (regional or worldwide) audience.[55] The present scenario brings a bigger challenge before the defence organisations in terms of handling new media technologies, in the backdrop of its exponential reach, impact and the way in which the 'user' content generated on these platforms can be distorted, manipulated and circulated to millions in an instant, which can be used by the enemy to its advantage. The usage of new media technology like in the Israeli-Hezbollah War of 2006 to, in recent times, the Islamic State of Iraq and the Levant social media campaign provides us an example of how the current information environment has impacted the way warfare is conducted today.[56]

In order to get information dominance in any given environment, undermining the importance and strength of new media can prove detrimental to the defence forces. There is an immediate need to understand the 'new media' as a concept, its technological dimensions, its impact and set of challenges and prospects. In addition, there is a requirement to optimise new media technologies and synchronise them with the aims and objectives of the military so that it can counter the adversaries' use of new media and subvert their aim. One w example of this is the recent creation of a special force of 'Facebook warriors' in the British Army, especially designed to undertake psychological operations and use of social media to engage in unconventional warfare in the information age. The 77th

Brigade, to be based in Hermitage, near Newbury, in Berkshire, is about 1,500-strong and formed of units drawn from across the army. The brigade will be responsible for the non-lethal warfare in the backdrop of 24-hour news, smartphones and social media, such as Facebook and Twitter.[57]

The employment of this strategy by British defence forces not only highlights the growing importance of new media in military operations but also underlines the fact that adversaries are using the new platforms to their advantage. It also accentuates the immediate need to review the potential of new media and advocate changes in the stance of the defence forces the way they have been previously viewing media and its impact. For a better understanding, let's examine some popular new media and how they have been exploited by various terrorist organisations time and again:

- **Abuse of Internet:** The Internet has been the first casualty in the new media technology, which has been continuously abused by the terrorist organizations and adversaries to their advantage. Ban Ki-moon, Secretary-General of the United Nations, said, "The Internet is a prime example of how terrorists can behave in a truly transnational way; in response, States need to think and function in an equally transnational manner."[58] It is important to note that the World Wide Web, as a subset of the Internet, is essentially ungoverned, providing obvious freedoms and cautions. The web gives the individual a voice, often an anonymous voice ... and a potentially vast audience.[59] This anonymity and unregulated freedom have been regularly exploited by the enemy, in terms of using the Internet for their own communication, false propaganda, raise funds, lure people to join their network, coordinating attacks, money laundering, using geo-tags, Google Earth for mapping, data collection, etc.
- **Abuse of Websites and Blogs:** As new media technologies become easier and cheaper to use, in terms of creation, content consumption, revamping and deleting the websites have become easier than ever. This facility has given terrorist organisations easier ways to communicate from unknown locations to huge masses, surpassing geographical locations and time zones. Websites are easily established, dismantled

and reestablished, making them valuable to extremist movements. Islamic extremist websites grew from twenty to over 4,000 in only five years.[60] The enemies can use these websites as virtual training grounds, offering tutorials on building ammunition like bombs, assist as a guide in how to use weapons at their disposal, shooting at soldiers, and sneaking into prone areas from abroad, host messages and propaganda videos which help to raise morale and further the expansion of recruitment and fundraising networks.[61]

- **Abuse of YouTube:** YouTube can empower individuals to achieve strategic political and military effects where easy upload of their videos, without editorial oversight, allows access to a nearly unlimited audience. Thus, the use of the improvised explosive device (IED) by insurgents shifts from a military tactical weapon to a strategic information weapon when the IED detonator is accompanied by a videographer.[62] But the question is if these platforms are continuously used by the terrorist organisation to do terror propaganda, then why are they allowed to put these videos in the first case? The answer can be summarized in two points, first is the lack of will to do so. Despite the serious threat posed by extreme and violent videos, neither the big Internet companies nor the European Union appears willing to take on a legal battle to enforce their removal.[63] Second, the videos on YouTube in terms of data are colossal, 'about 300 hours of video material is being uploaded to YouTube every minute, making it virtually impossible for the company to filter all images.' Internet giant Google accepted the fact that its video-sharing website YouTube is so inundated that staff cannot filter all terror related content, complicating the struggle to halt the publication of terrorist propaganda and hostage videos.[64]

To conclude, new media is one of the main forces in accelerating the trend of globalisation in human society.[65] Due to the thrust of new media, the global trend creates new social networks and activities, redefines political, cultural, economic, geographical and other boundaries of human society, expands and stretches social relations, intensifies and accelerates social exchanges,[66] and involves both the micro-structures of personhood and macro-structures of the community.[67] Given its indispensable nature, unchallenging presence, infinite reach, deep impact, it becomes paramount for the defence organisation to understand it from the core and optimise its potentials for achieving the military objective.

The article was originally published on the Centre for Air Power Studies (CAPS) website

9

Application of Social Media by Defence Personnel for Personal Use

Today, with the advancement in communication technologies, the virtual reality of social media has started to blur the boundaries between the real and virtual worlds. This not only brings with it new opportunities, but also different challenges. One such challenge is being faced by the organisations which are involved in various critical areas, especially the security of the country. This article is important for those social media users who are working for the critical organisations like defence, or attached to them directly or indirectly. Although use of social media, is debated a lot, but one has to bear in mind the abuses also. Following are some suggestions:

- Whatever you share as an update, be it on any social media platform you are making the message viral to all those known and "unknown" people who are connected to you directly or indirectly or, just by virtue of being a social media user. Any information on matters related to the organisation (Text, audio, videos) should not be shared on these platforms. A trivial piece of information may be of no relevance to you but can be the last piece of information required for "unwarranted" elements to complete a jigsaw puzzle.
- It is also not advisable to share your locations, frequent places of your visits, etc., on social media because by sharing these locations as a user, you might think there is no harm but for "unwarranted" elements it is easier to profile your day to day activities and places of your interest.
- Social media has one tempting button of "share" which needs to be used with "caution". Do not share any news items, or content designed

like news items without verifying its authenticity. The authenticity can be checked through the search engine of news websites. There are numerous stories, which go viral and users continue to share it without confirming its authenticity.

- One of the advices given by Lisa Respers France, senior producer for CNN Digital's Entertainment section is that, "stop believing everything you see online. From Facebook privacy fakes to Twitter death hoaxes, think before you share that link. Every time you post the story you legitimise it. Also check the dates of the story.... Here my rules for you, if you are going to share something 'Stop, Drop and Roll'. 'Stop' before you hit that share button, 'drop' over Google and 'roll' around the information there."[68]
- Be extremely careful with the viral hoax floating on social media platforms, especially Facebook. Sometimes these hoax news are pure, mischievous scaremongering, but some Facebook hoaxes were more malign: bait to get people to click through to malware-ridden websites. In January 2015, Facebook decided to annotate suspicious stories with a warning, but maintains it's still a platform not a publisher. Now the social network is cracking down with changes to its news feed that will ensure its users see fewer hoax and spam posts, while providing a warning of their potential falsity when they are seen.[69]
- Social media has unquestionably altered the nature of private and public communication, which one has to bear in mind while using social media tools and applications.[70] Gagging and denial is not an answer. But to be careful with the economy of information passing on these platforms will be a right step in this direction. Instead of sharing personal information where it is visible to all, it is better to inbox your message or shoot off an email.
- Build your own social media policy and make sure you involve all stakeholders in it.

What's the Way Out?

- Shunning the personnel is not an answer neither the gagging.
- Awareness about the lurking dangers on the social media platforms

needs to be emphasised. Instead of making it an order of the day it should be incorporated in the lifestyle of the personnel.

- Information related to Defence personnel, personal life, families, posting details, unit details, troops location and movements, selfies giving away the location landmark or equipment, or details of inventory, telephones, mobile numbers should not be shared on social media platforms.
- A practical and empathetic social media policy is required which can balance between the organisation's sensitivities and personnel sensitivities.

Defence forces have continuously tried to evolve themselves, with the changing times, technologies and the threat which emerges from the changing technologies. Communication technologies in general and media in specific are always evolving which does bring lots of challenges before the Defence organisations. Social media and its tools are another challenge but if tapped it can be utilised in a manner beneficial to the organisation.

The article was originally published on the Centre for Air Power Studies (CAPS) website

10

Application of Media Dependency Theory during Crisis: Op *MEGH RAHAT*

Communication in general and mass communication in particular plays an indispensable role in our everyday lives. However, their importance grows manifolds during crisis situations. According to the dictionary, " crisis is a condition of instability or danger, as in social, economic, political, or international affairs, leading to a decisive change." Natural disasters fall in this category.

During a natural disaster, apart from other social institutions, which work to manage the disaster, the functioning of media becomes crucial. The key role of the media is informing the people and the authorities during emergencies. Media plays a vital role in public awareness and preparedness through educating the public about disasters; warning of hazards; gathering and transmitting information about affected areas; alerting government officials, helping relief organisations and the public towards specific needs; and even in facilitating discussions about disaster preparedness and response. During any emergency, people seek up-to date, reliable and detailed information.[71]

Amid crisis the media also integrate with other social systems working towards disaster management. Simultaneously, social institutions act as a source of first hand information for the media. Therefore, we witness a scene where multi social institutions depend on each other to inform the masses, save lives, mobilise the man and the material and above all attain the common objective of saving lives and bringing back equilibrium to society which is hit by a natural calamity.

In the recent past, India witnessed floods in Jammu and Kashmir, which not only claimed more than 400 lives, but also displaced thousands of people and left behind a trail of destruction. According to the Press Trust of India, "The floods caused havoc across many districts of the state in which over 15 lakh families spread over 5,794 villages were affected. As per the assessment received, around 3,44,607 structures have suffered damages, 90,000 cattle and other livestock perished, crop loss reported in 6.52 lakh hectares of land besides huge loss to public and private infrastructure."

In a bid to save precious lives, the relief and rescue work done by the Indian Army, under the name of Operation *Megh Rahat* deserves special mention. Op *Megh Rahat* commenced on 2 September 2014 and ended on September 19, 2014. During the two-week long operation more than 2,00,000 flood affected people were rescued by the Indian Armed forces from the various parts of the flood-hit state.

The recent natural calamity provides an insight to understand the role of media better and to see its functioning with other social institutions in general, and the military in particular. If one sees 'Operation *Megh Rahat*' from the lens of media studies, it emerges as a fair example of Media Dependency theory. The central point of the theory states that people in modern society depend on the media to comprehend and understand the world around them. Melvin Defleur and Sandra Ball-Rokeach developed this basic idea in the mid-1970s; though the theory has fallen out of favour today, the central tenets of the work still hold true in post-modern society. The basis of the dependency theory is what Defleur and Ball-Rokeach call an 'ecological' model. In this, they see a complex web of links with the mass media and the public at large.[72]

During the floods, we saw how the Indian Army utilised (depended) on various media platforms, especially the social media and was able to connect to the 'public at large'. The Army largely depended on the media to disseminate information to the masses with regard to ongoing natural calamity and rescue operations and was also able to promote their point of view to the masses. Moreover, we also saw how for the first time, the Indian Army used the social media platform like Facebook, Twitter,

WhatsApp, to provide instant information to the general masses. An Indian army official stated, "An estimated 12,000 people were assisted on the basis of reports received over the social media." In addition to this, we also saw how the media's need for the first hand information on the floods was catered by the armed forces. This dependency reinforces the Defleur and Ball Rokeach views that even though the 'parts may depend on each other, it is a kind of an ecological relationship, not one amongst equals, that forms the dependency relationship.' The media and military are two different entities, with different objectives, different styles of working but still the dependency exist. So, one can say that the media military relationship becomes more important and challenging during the crisis situation.

Moreover, one of the key ideas of the media dependency theory is that the 'Social institutions and media systems interact with audiences to create needs, interests, and motives in the person.' Social institutions, which are established sets of norms and subsystems, support each society's survival. Each sector carries out certain tasks and has different responsibilities that contribute to the overall functioning and stability of a society.[73] The military is also one such institution and coverage of Op *Megh Rahat* by the media and utilisation of media tools by military, depicts how different social institutions and media systems interact and inform the masses at the time of crisis. It also depicts how people who may not be directly linked to the present disaster were motivated and mobilised to be a part of the rescue work and its aftermath, largely due to media.

The article was originally published on the Centre for Air Power Studies (CAPS) website

11

Poland's New Media Law and its Implication on Polish Press Freedom

A vibrant civil society can challenge those in power by documenting corruption or uncovering activities like the murder of political enemies. In democracies, this function is mostly performed by the media, NGOs or opposition parties.

– Evgeny Morozov

Recently, Poland, the East European country located near the Baltic Sea, was in the news for several reasons, including the controversial media law passed by the ruling Polish government. This article is an attempt to present a brief overview of Poland's political milieu and media landscape, Poland's contemporary status; related to the press freedom and freedom of expression, to discuss the Polish journalism philosophy and to bring to light the details of recent controversial media law signed by the ruling party and its implication on Warsaw media and freedom of expression.

Present Political Milieu

The present political setup of Republic of Poland is based on parliamentary republic or parliamentary constitutional republic based on parliamentary system resting on the four pillars of executive, legislature, judiciary and press (as the fourth pillar or estate). The decisive Warsaw parliamentary elections held in October 2015 brought in power Poland's far-right Law and Justice party (PiS). At present it has its domination in both the houses and is headed by the sixteenth Prime Minister Beata Szydło, who also happens to be the third woman premier of the country and first to triumph over the serving woman PM Ewa Kopacz in 2015. Andrzej Duda from the Law and Justice party is the President of the Republic of Poland.

Polish Media Landscape in Brief

With literacy rate of 99.8 per cent (as per UNESCO Institute for Statistics), the total number of daily newspapers in Poland is approximately 59, which covers approximately 3,86,33,912 of Polish dominated population. Accounted as one of the most populated countries in the European Union, there are around 179 TV stations, 792 Radio Stations, approximately 35,83,620 of Cable Subscribers, 25,00,000 of Satellite Subscribers and around 28,00,000 individuals with Internet access respectively.[74] From media consumption perspective, the post-industrial Polish society is more 'television-centric society' and relies intensively on use of electronic media like television for entertainment in comparison to newspaper; therefore, Poland has low newspaper circulation. The present Polish media has evolved from the 1989 communist collapse. A strong characteristic of Polish newspapers is that they do not attempt to disguise their political sympathies and readers can expect the opinions of editors to be explicitly expressed. In addition, Polish papers often do not separate news from opinions.[75]

Poland's Contemporary Status related to the Press Freedom and Freedom of Expression

The Freedom of the Press 2015 positioned Poland at 47th number in its annual global media freedom report. According to Reporters Without Borders, Poland is ranked at 18th position out of 180 countries in the 2015 World Press Freedom Index with score of 12.71. In more than a decade long journey it has come from 58th position in 2005 to 18th position in 2015, indicating a conducive environment for free press to flourish. However, the year 2015 also stunned the Poland media organisations by the deadly assault leading to the slaying of 31-year-old Journalist Lukasz Masiak, known for his news reports on controversial issues. The killing of Masiak again reignited the debate on the security of journalists in Poland in general and European Union in particular. In response to the incident,

Censorship CEO Jodie Ginsberg noted that, "Media workers in Europe are facing an increased level of violence as they do their jobs. We call on the European Union and governments across the continent to mount a concerted effort to protect press freedom and the lives of media workers by aggressively pursuing threats of violence against journalists ... Index has been tracking threats to journalists across Europe for more than a year, through our Mapping Media Freedom project, and have noted a worrying trend of violence towards the sector."[76]

The history of Poland has traces of censorship prior to the fall of communalism but subsequently it changed with passing of anti-censorship act in 1990s. Later on with emergence of privatisation, foreign investors in media and new communication and media technology, it lead to further diminishing of government's influence on Polish media, which the recent law has challenged. The recent happenings in Poland have also got severe criticism from all quarters of the world, especially the media organisations.

Another observation, which needs to be mentioned at this point, is that there is an increase in the number of defamation suits brought annually by government officials and public figures against news media. Also, there have been relatively few investigations or charges in recent years under the so-called blasphemy law restricting speech that causes religious offense, but the provision remains a highly criticised constraint on freedom of expression in Poland.[77]

Polish Journalism Philosophy

From the reference frame of Fred S. Siebert, Theodore Peterson and Wilbur Schramm, *Four Theories of the Press* the Polish journalism philosophy is based on Libertarian theory of press. From theoretical perspective, the Poland media and journalism is based on free press theory of normative media theory. Free press theory proclaims complete freedom of public expression and of economic operation of the media and rejects any interference by government in any aspect of the press. A well-functioning market should resolve all issues of media obligation and social need.[78]

Poland's Controversial Media Law

On the eve of New Year the ruling government, despite concerns conveyed by the European Union, passed an amendment to existing Warsaw's media law. As per the government, it is an attempt to 'depoliticise the airwaves' and the intention of the new media bill is to revamp the existing state run broadcasters and news agencies in Poland. However, the move is seen as the government's attempt to rein in the press. The new bill bestows power to the new ruling government to 'appoint heads of public television and radio, as well as civil services.' The new power gives the recently elected government political control over the Warsaw state media, thus influencing and to an extent challenging the status of free press in Poland.

The move is under lot of criticism from the media organisations, journalist fraternity, European Union and Polish populace. It was also criticised by the European Broadcasting Union (EBU). Prior to the passing of the Bill EBU Director General, Ingrid Deltenre wrote a letter addressed to the Polish President Andrzej Duda and noted that, "To preserve the integrity and independence of public service media as a symbol of a free and democratic country, we ask you in the strongest possible terms not to sign this measure into law."[79] The European Federation of Journalists (EFJ) labeled the new law as newly elected conservative government's attempt to exert more control on public service broadcasting media and to "repolonise" print media.[80]

However, in response to European Union commission criticism, the Polish authorities have 'fired back, angrily dismissing the criticism and complaining that European officials are meddling in their affairs.' While defending the government's stance, Polish Deputy Prime Minister and Culture Minister, Piotr Glinski noted that, 'a new media law shall be adopted in the next two months in order to "transform" the public media ... that public service television (TVP), public service radio (PR) – including 17 regional radio programmes and the national press agency (PAP) – shall be transformed into "national cultural institutions", under the control of the Culture Minister.'[81]

To conclude, this 'transformation' of Polish media reignites the debate of the press liberty and freedom of expression, which are the essential elements of robust democracy. In the present scenario, it is for sure that the ruling government will be deciding the parameters of this 'transformation' and as the events unfold themselves, the implications of this transformation will be visible. Nevertheless, the uproar over the recent episode in itself presents how sensitive the issue is and how fragile Poland's environment has become for free press to flourish. With coming of the government control we will be witnessing the shift happening in the Polish media and in its journalism philosophy. And most likely the 'transformed' Polish media will be influenced by the ruling government ideology dominated by the Kaczyńskis' conservative law and order agenda and soft Eurosceptic[82] or Anti-EUism. The new law is detrimental to the democratic values and not in sync with the spirit of European Union. Will the Polish people let the hard-earned democracy and its elements like press freedom and freedom of expression get diluted in the present political milieu, would be an interesting development to be watched in coming times?

The paper was originally published Eupheus – An International Refereed Research Journal (Multidisciplinary Quarterly) ISSN 2348-9774.

12

Online News Reporting of Massive Ordnance Air Blast in Afghanistan:
A Battle of Narratives

On April 13, 2017, as the news broke that the United States of America (USA) has dropped its GBU-43/B/Massive Ordnance Air Blast (MOAB), also known as "Mother of All Bombs", on the eastern Nangarhar province of Afghanistan, the explosion not only rattled the war-torn mountains but also sent a shockwave in the newsrooms across the globe. The most lethal non-nuclear weapon was ordained to obliterate the underground tunnels labyrinth used by Islamic State of Iraq and Syria (ISIS).

MOAB was dropped by the U.S. Air Force Special Operations command MC-130. The super bomb, a 22,600 lbs weapon with 18,700 lbs of H-6 explosive filler, is an inertially guided weapon that relies on the Global Positioning System (GPS) course corrections. The weapon is extensively used in regions where spaces are confined, like caves or canyons.[83]

The strike also bombarded the global news media with colossal news reports in the digital world, which churned out stories on the various specifications, trajectory, weight, history, etc. about the bomb. The narratives were constructed around the reactions of various world leaders, questions on the future of the ISIS, impact of strike on other conflicts like North Korea, Syria, US & Russia relationship, etc. The objective of this article is to shed light on how various online news media reacted to the MOAB strike on the day it happened. The scope of the article only confines itself to the first 24 hours of news reports and analysis of one or two online news report samples disseminated by different countries online news agencies/news websites.

USA

FoxNews and CNN highlighted the specification of the MOAB in detail; it also spoke about the psychological impact of the weapon. The narrative adopted by Fox was to display the lethality of the weapon and projecting the "shock and awe" on the adversary. An article titled "*The 'Mother of All Bombs' (MOAB) has been dropped on Afghanistan. Here's what it does (and doesn't) mean*," carried by FoxNews written by Lt. General, Thomas W. Spoehr, Director of The Heritage Foundation's Center for National Defense, USA who spoke about how the present strike was in continuation of the US' older strategy which has just been taken forward by the existing Trump administration, with no intent to escalate the matter, but only to use the right ammunition according to the desired target.[84]

Russia

Contrary to the US media stance, the Russian Sputnik news agency article, "*Washington's Weapon of Mass Destruction Not Scaring Anybody*," made the following observations: Sputnik carried the views of Greg Mello of the Los Alamos Study Group, who labeled MOAB as an "an obsolete and ineffective bomb," used only as a "psychological wêapon" which "makes a propaganda point". The timing was also interesting as Mello reveals that the "show of force was used just hours after the Pentagon admitted that one of their airstrikes in Syria had mistakenly killed 18 of our so-called rebels."[85] It also questioned if the US President Trump even gave a nod to it or it was the Commander of the US forces in Afghanistan Gen. John Nicolson's decision to go ahead? The Sputnik also undermined the latest move by the US while taking views of military experts and underscored that the recent show of strength by the US will have no significant impact on the war in Afghanistan.[86]

China

The official mouth-piece of Chinese government, Xinhua initially reported of the strike on the similar lines as the western media and shared the statement from the Pentagon that, "The strike was designed to minimise the risk to Afghan and U.S. Forces conducting clearing operations in the area while maximising the destruction of ISIS-Khorasan fighters and facilities."[87] It also presented the press conference by Gen. John Nicholson as he was defending the timing and motive behind the strike. An article by Editor Mengjiao Liu deserves attention here, as it talks about Russian senator Igor Morozov RIA news agency's quote that, "The U.S. test of the new bomb in Afghanistan is an attempt to establish world dominance with an element of a military threat which may initiate a new round of arms race and increase tension in the world."[88] However, China's own reaction was still awaited.

Middle East

Doha-based Al Jazeera news gave an extensive coverage to the strike. The initial report presented the Pentagon's statements and hinted that, "ultra-heavy explosive – equal to 11 tonnes of TNT with a blast radius of 1.6 km on each side – could potentially cause many civilian casualties."[89] It also mentioned the rationale behind using the MOAB, confusion behind who gave the orders, and estimated ISIS strength in Afghanistan around 1500 fighters. It concluded with a video, which exhibited how ISIL are recruiting and brainwashing Afghan children.[90] It also voiced the former Afghan President Hamid Karzai's condemnation to the strike.[91] It also shared President Karzai's Twitter posts where he tweeted, "This is not the war on terror but the inhuman and most brutal misuse of our country as testing ground for new and dangerous weapons."[92] The same was resonant in the tweets of Afghan envoy to Pakistan, Omar Zakhilwal, who tweeted; "I find the use of the largest non-nuclear bomb, the so called 'mother of all bombs', on our soil reprehensible & counterproductive."[93]

Afghanistan

The official state news agency of the war-ravaged country, Bakhtar News Agency, reported that 36 ISIS 'affiliated' casualties, no civilian casualties and acceptance that Afghan government was well aware of the upcoming strike. It also shared the U.S. Forces-Afghanistan Commander General John Nicholson's statement and spoke about the 'atrocities' committed by ISIS in the region and the US resolve to support Afghanistan. [94]

ISIS

A statement published by the ISIS mouthpiece, "Amaq News Agency" denied any casualty from its side. Amaq also published an infographic downplaying the impact of the MOAB.[95]

Fig 1: Infographic by Amaq[96]

To conclude, the online news media was engulfed with MOAB strike as it happened and presented before us how the digital media reacted to a major event and how narratives and counter-narratives were built in a minimum time. The scope of the article limits itself to just provide a glimpse of how the online news media reported. Based on the miniscule sample taken from various online news media outlets of different countries allowed on Google (India), the article finds different narratives and counter-narratives getting constructed in the digital news sphere. Where western online news media projected it as a chest-thumping event for the US, the Russians undermined the entire strike, while China treaded with caution by only giving views of the Russians. The Japanese Kyodonews website, after five days of the strike, just had a passing reference about the strike,[97] without naming MOAB, but quoting U.S. Vice President Mike Pence's warning to North Korea.[98] On the contrary, the Middle East provided an extensive coverage of the event. However, the ground zero reportage from Afghanistan was the only news report with missing analysis, and defying every narrative, while the ISIS completely denied the claims made by the entire world.

The paper was originally published then UGC Approved journal Adroitic – An International Refereed Research Journal (Multidisciplinary) ISSN: 2349-6274.

13

Paris Attacks from the Prism of Social Media

Innovations in communication technologies have transformed the very way in which we promulgate, disseminate and share information. These communication technologies are so much integrated in our lifestyles that gradually our survival relies heavily on them. However, the ease and comfort which these technologies provide us, in terms of connectivity, sharing of messages, uninterrupted and interminable means of communication, has also started to pose severe challenges for us, which to some extent can bring pandemonium in our society, thus defeating the very rationale behind the creation of media, to bind people and make informed society with enlightened minds.

One such example that demands our immediate attention is the use of social media where the boundaries between the users and producers have blurred, the information checks and balances have reduced and the spread of the information has compressed time, nationality, distance boundaries, and now messages can reach millions of people in less than a second, depending on the bandwidth or internet speed.

The dream of connecting people to communicate and make the society informed is gradually making society ill-informed, thriving on unverified information, mis-information, manipulated information with hidden agendas by group of few individuals with their own motives and above all more insensitive towards each other at times.

From the media perspective, the recent November Paris attacks, which left around 130 dead, several injured, has not only reignited the debates at various levels, but also have again raised the question about the very use and abuse of social media. The ill-fated event also presented before us another example how the social media platform used by millions, connected by millions has made the situation, especially crisis situation, more complicated.

Where on one hand social media twitter handles of various news channels like Reuters, Associated Press (AP), Agence France-Presse (AFP), World news, etc. were disseminating minute-to-minute details of the attack, international reaction towards the carnage, YouTube showed videos of rescue work, and Twitter forwarded human interest tweets like "*France 24 reports Paris taxi drivers have switched off meters, taking people home for free*".[99] The social media platform was also used by embassies to assist their people, and more importantly how terror stricken people were trying to locate their loves ones, warn other fellow countrymen to stay away from the terror attack affected areas to which they were witness, displayed how social media aspect of mass media lived up to its 'creator's' vision behind creating it. Another trend, which needs to be highlighted at this point, is how social media like Facebook and Twitter transformed itself as per the crisis and provided 'safety tools' like 'safety check' to its users so that they can communicate about their well-being to their families.

But on other hand we also saw the abuse of social media by certain sections of users who used the social media platform to instigate people, legitimise lashing of particular community or region, hidden political motive, hoodwink youth in name of religion and instigate them to be part of terrorist activities, etc. If we see the negative dimension of the Paris attack from social media perspective, we will observe how the social media platform was abused by certain individuals to bring forward their own agenda using the ill-fated event for their personal gain along with the 'insensitivity' and 'dumbing down quality of debates' which was witnessed on social media platforms. We saw how US presidential election 2016 candidate Republican Donald John Trump's insensitive remarks on twitter like "*Isn't it interesting that the tragedy in Paris took place in one of the toughest gun control countries in the world?*" The remark did bring fury of *Twitterati* on social media. Another tweet by Trump, which again faced the *Twitterati* outrage, was "*If the people so violently shot down in Paris had guns, at least they would have had a fighting chance*",[100] thus using the Paris massacre as a platform to legitimise and propagate hoarding of weapons and practice of violence instead of finding minimum collateral damage or an amicable solution. This was followed by another US Republican politician Jeff Duncan's insensitive remark and equally insensitive juxtaposition in response to the Paris attack. In one of his tweets, Duncan wrote, "*How's that Syrian refugee resettlement look now? How about that mass migration into Europe?*[101] *Terrorism is alive & well in the world. #No.*"That's another debate who funded the terrorist group? As the real truth behind the creation of ISIS and middle east crisis is pointing towards west, the reports which are been brought to light by media cites that MI6 had cooperated with the CIA on a "rat line" of arms transfers from Libyan stockpiles to the Syrian rebels in 2012 after the fall of the Gaddafi regime.[102] The decisions by west have resulted into one of the major human displacement issues, which, at the time of Paris attack was mocked by the western politicians only. This again reveals the lack of will to accept the blunder, resolve the crisis and using media to propagate the weapon culture where the ultimate beneficiary will be the manufacturers of the weapons at the cost of human lives.

These examples are advance warnings for us on how everything on social media cannot be taken lightly, how the messages floating within a second can be a hidden propaganda technique used to cover the real truth, hoodwink the users and knowingly and unknowingly using our personal social media platforms to work as vehicles to propagate those ideas thus 'manufacturing a world of lies' to which we also become part of when we blindly 'like' or 'share' them. Today, with a single reasonably priced smart phone and Internet connection, an amateur can produce an uncensored content and viral it to millions with a click of a mouse, or just a touch. Or just with posting unverified information can instigate, misinform or confuse masses. So do these challenges defeat the very purpose of the creators of social media or do these incidents set an example for us to understand the use of social media and to what extent it can be abused so that we can form proper guidelines to use it and achieve the ambition of well informed society? The answer lies in understanding the impact of the use and abuse of the social media by society. If a technology is challenging the very elements which bind the society in harmony and peace, then it's high time to put checks and balances in place. One of the checks and balances start at the individual level; only then it can spread at the social level. And to begin with the Mahatma Gandhi's Three Wise Monkey story, "*See no Evil, Hear No Evil, Speak No Evil*" can be further modified with the changing times to "*Tweet no evil, share no evil and like no evil.*" The intent is not to turn blind to evil, but not to let evil enter and circulate in the system.

The paper was originally published then UGC Approved journal Adroitic –An International Refereed Research Journal (Multidisciplinary) ISSN: 2349-6274.

Notes

1. "Who Coined the Term "Virtual Reality"?" Virtual Reality. 2015. http://www.vrs.org.uk/virtual-reality/who-coined-the-term.html. Accessed on October 30, 2015.
2. Ingram, Mathew. "New York Times Enters the World of Virtual Reality with Google Partnership." *Fortune*, October 20, 2015. http://fortune.com/2015/10/20/nyt-google-cardboard/. Accessed on November 5, 2015.
3. Terdiman, Daniel. "Virtual Reality Journalism Is Coming to the Associated Press." Fast Company. November 5, 2015. http://www.fastcompany.com/3053219/fast-feed/virtual-reality-journalism-is-coming-to-the-associated-press. Accessed November 8, 2015.
4. http://www.slashgear.com/google-cardboard-gets-serious-vr-headsets-for-the-masses-10359008/
5. http://www.cnet.com/news/googles-cardboard-vr-headset-is-no-joke-its-great-for-the-oculus-rift/
6. Dash, Leon. "Immersion Journalism." Open School of Journalism. http://www.openschoolofjournalism.com/distance-education-program/courses/immersion-journalism-jg190. Accessed on November 7, 2015.
7. n. 2.
8. n. 3.
9. Somaiya, Ravi. "The Times Partners With Google on Virtual Reality Project." *New York Times.* October 21, 2015. http://www.nytimes.com/2015/10/21/business/media/the-times-partners-with-google-on-virtual-reality-project.html. Accessed October 31, 2015.
10. Ibid.
11. Drone strikes in Pakistan.John Brennan marks first year at CIA amid no confirmed civilian drone deaths in Pakistan.11 March 2014. http://www.thebureauinvestigates.com/2014/03/11/john-brennan-marks-first-year-at-cia-amid-no-confirmed-civilian-drone-deaths-in-pakistan/. Accessed on March 12, 2014.
12. The Drone Wars. Weapons like the Predator kill far fewer civilians. January 9, 2010. http://online.wsj.com/news/articles/SB10001424052748704130904574644632368664254. Accessed on March 12, 2014.
13. Ibid.
14. Jones, Steve. "Introduction." In *Encyclopedia of New Media: An Essential Reference to Communication and Technology*, 1. New York: Sage Publications, 2002.
15. Marvin, Carolyn. "Introduction." In *When Old Technologies Were New: Thinking About Electric Communication in the Late Nineteenth Century: Thinking About Electric Communication in the Late Nineteenth Century*, 3. Madison Avenue, New York: Oxford University Press, 1998.
16. n. 1.

17. McLuhan, M. and Q. Fiore. (1967). T*he Medium is the Massage: An Inventory of Effects*. Co-ordinated by J. Agel. New York, London, Toronto: Bantam Books.
18. Levinson, Paul. "Through a Glass, Brightly." In *Digital McLuhan: A Guide to the Information Millennium*, 174. New York: Taylor & Francis, 1999.
19. "Definition of New Media." Ziff Davis, LLC. PCMag Digital Group. http://www.pcmag.com/encyclopedia/term/47936/new-media. Accessed on July 24, 2014.
20. Jenkins, Henry. "Introduction." In *Convergence Culture: Where Old and New Media Collide*, 10. New York: New York University Press, 2006.
21. "ComScore Releases the "2013 India Digital Future in Focus" Report." ComScore. August 22, 2013. https://www.comscore.com/Insights/Press-Releases/2013/8/comScore-Releases-the-2013-India-Digital-Future-in-Focus-Report. Accessed on June 11, 2014.
22. ComScore is a leading internet technology company that measures what people do as they navigate the digital world – and turns that information into insights and actions for our clients to maximise the value of their digital investments.
23. Schwittay, Anke. "New Media Practices in India: Bridging Past and Future, Markets and Development." *International Journal of Communication* 5, no. 20110349 (2011): 348.
24. n. 12, p. 352.
25. Ravindran, G. (2008). The cultural politics of new media modernity in India: Reading the roles of moral panic agents and mobile phone Users. Paper presented at International Workshop on ICTs and Development: Experiences from Asia. National University of Singapore, Singapore.
26. n. 12, p. 350.
27. Information and Communication Technologies for Development.
28. n. 15.
29. Schwarzenegger, Christian. 'Exploring Digital Yesterdays – Reflections On New Media And The Future Of Communication'. *Historical Social Research* 37, no. 4 (2012): 118.
30. "Press Council of India Report on Paid News." Press Council of India (PCI). July 30, 2010. http://presscouncil.nic.in/OldWebsite/CouncilReport.pdf. The author has referred to this report while writing this article. Accessed on January 14, 2015.
31. Rouse, Margaret. "Social Engineering." From the Essential Guide: How to Hone an Effective Vulnerability Management Program. January 1, 2014. http://searchsecurity.techtarget.com/definition/social-engineering. Accessed on February 21, 2015.
32. SANS paper "The Threat of Social Engineering and your defence against it." 2003.
33. Foster, James. "A CISO's Nightmare: Digital Social Engineering." Securityweek Network: Information Security News. January 12, 2015. http://www.securityweek.com/cisos-nightmare-digital-social-engineering. Accessed on February 21, 2015.
34. The Official World Wide Web Anniversary Site.
35. Darnay, Keith. "Terrorism Is Going Digital." Bismarck Tribune. June 13, 2011. http://bismarcktribune.com/news/columnists/keith-darnay/terrorism-is-going-digital/article_e5ddc9ae-938a-11e0-bded-001cc4c03286.html. Accessed on February 14, 2015.

36. Mahan, Sue, and Pamala L. Griset. "The Internet and Terrorism." In *Terrorism in Perspective*, 282. California: Sage Publications, 2013.
37. Fischer, Robert. "Terrorism as Tool of Destruction." In *Introduction to Security*, 376. 7th ed. Burlington: Butterworth-Heinemann, 2004.
38. Von Behr, Ines, Anaïs Reding, Charlie Edwards, and Luke Gribbon. "Radicalisation in the Digital Era: The Use of the Internet in 15 Cases of Terrorism and Extremism." 2013. http://www.rand.org/content/dam/rand/pubs/research_reports/RR400/RR453/RAND_RR453.pdf. Accessed on February 14, 2015.
39. Joseph S. Nye, Jr. Soft Power, Hard Power and Leadership. http://www.hks.harvard.edu/netgov/files/talks/docs/11_06_06_seminar_Nye_HP_SP_Leadership.pdf. Assessed on June 20, 2014.
40. Soft Power. Oxford University Press (2014). http://www.oxforddictionaries.com/definition/english/soft-power. Accessed on June 25, 2014.
41. Geun Lee, *A Theory of Soft Power in International Politics: A Preliminary Attempt in Korean,* Kukje Jiyeok Yongu,Spring, 2004, pp. 1-18.
42. n. 39.
43. Ying Fan, "Soft Power: Power of Attraction or Confusion? Place Branding and Public Diplomacy" (Brunel Business School, Brunel University 2008). http://bura.brunel.ac.uk/bitstream/2438/1594/3/FullText.pdf. Accessed on June 20, 2014.
44. Geun Lee. A *Theory of Soft Power and Korea's Soft Power Strategy*, Seoul National University, p. 3.
45. Nachman Shai is an Israeli journalist and politician who currently serves as a member of the Knesset. He previously worked as the IDF spokesman.
46. Media plays large role in shift from hard to soft power, says Knesset member Nachman Shai. http://shorensteincenter.org/2014/04/nachman-shai/. Accessed on June 23, 2014.
47. Media in the South. http://hermanwasserman.wordpress.com/2013/09/17/the-media-as-a-vehicle-for-chinas-soft-power/. Accessed on July 7, 2014.
48. Daya Kishan Thussu. *Communicating India's Soft Power: Buddha to Bollywood* (New York: Palgrave Macmillan, 2013), p. 2.
49. 'Can India become a great power?', *The Economist*, March 30, 2013. http://www.economist.com/news/leaders/21574511-indias-lack-strategic-culture-hobbles-its-ambition-be-force-world-can-india. Accessed on June 22, 2014.
50. n. 48.
51. Press Release. FICCI-KPMG Report 2013. https://www.kpmg.com/IN/en/Press%20Release/FICCI-KPMG%20Press%20Release.pdf. Accessed on June 20, 2014.
52. FICCI FRAMES 2014: Indian Media Industry Contributes 0.5% Of GDP. *India Times.* 13 March 2014.
53. n. 51.
54. Shikha Dalmia. Bollywood's Soft Power (2012). http://www.utne.com/arts/bollywoods-soft-power-cultural-war-on-extremism.aspx#ixzz3630FD74m. Accessed on June 20, 2014.

55. Murphy, Dennis M. "Introduction." In *Fighting Back: New Media and Military Operations*. (Pennsylvania: U.S. Army War College, 2008), p. 4.
56. Ibid.
57. MacAskill, Ewen. "British Army Creates Team of Facebook Warriors." *The Guardian*, January 31, 2015, UK News sec. http://www.theguardian.com/uk-news/2015/jan/31/british-army-facebook-warriors-77th-brigade. Accessed on May 18, 2015.
58. "The Use of the Internet for Terrorist Purposes." *United Nations Office on Drugs And Crime*, 2012. http://www.unodc.org/documents/frontpage/Use_of_Internet_for_Terrorist_Purposes.pdf. Accessed on May 18, 2015.
59. n. 55, p. 4.
60. Ibid.
61. Kaplan, Eben. "Terrorists and the Internet." *Council on Foreign Relations*. January 8, 2009. http://www.cfr.org/terrorism-and-technology/terrorists-internet/p10005. Accessed on May 17, 2015.
62. n. 55, p. 6.
63. "YouTube Too Overloaded to Filter Terrorist Videos." *Cbsnews.com*, January 28, 2015, News sec. http://www.cbsnews.com/news/youtube-too-overloaded-to-filter-terrorist-videos/. Accessed on May 19, 2015.
64. Ibid.
65. Chen, G. M., & Zhang, K. "New media and cultural identity in the global society". In R. Taiwo (Ed.), *Handbook of Research on Discourse Behavior and Digital Communication: Language Structures and Social Interaction*. (Hershey, PA: Idea Group Inc. 2010), pp. 801-815.
66. Chen, Guo-Ming. "The Impact Of New Media On Intercultural Communication in Global Context". *China Media Research* 8, no. 2 (2012): 1. http://digitalcommons.uri.edu/cgi/viewcontent.cgi?article=1012&context=com_facpubs. Accessed on March 11, 2015.
67. Steger, Manfred. "Globalization: A Contested Topic." In *Globalization: A Very Short Introduction*, 1st ed. (Oxford: Oxford University Press, 2013), p. 15.
68. Lisa Respers France. "No! Don't share this stuff online!." Edition.cnn.com.01.46. January 20, 2015. http://edition.cnn.com/videos/tech/2015/01/20/fake-stories-internet-psa-lisas-desk-orig-mg.cnn.
69. Dredge, Stuart. "Facebook Promises Less Hoax Stories and Spam Posts in Users' News Feeds." *The Guardian*, January 21, 2015, Technology sec. http://www.theguardian.com/technology/2015/jan/21/facebook-news-feed-hoaxes-spam. Accessed on May 21, 2015.
70. Dijck, José Van. "Engineering Sociality in a Culture of Connectivity." In *The Culture of Connectivity: A Critical History of Social Media*, 5. Madison Avenue: Oxford University Press, 2013.
71. "Role of Media in Disaster Management." National Institute of Disaster Management (NIDM). November 4, 2009. http://nidm.gov.in/idmc2/PDF/Concept/Media.pdf. Accessed on October 15, 2014.

72. McCallum, Michael. "The Dependency Theory of Mass Communication with Australian Examples." Academia.edu. January 1, 2013. http://www.academia.edu/2632078/The_Dependency_theory_of_Mass_Communication_with_Australian_Examples. Accessed July 30, 2014.
73. Devore, K. "Social Institutions: Definition, Examples & Quiz." Educational Portal. January 1, 2014.
74. "Poland Press, Media, TV, Radio, Newspapers Forum." *Pressreference*. http://www.pressreference.com/No-Sa/Poland.html. Accessed on January 12, 2016.
75. Ibid.
76. Lussier, Natalie. "Poland: Journalist Lukasz Masiak Fatally Beaten." Indexcensorship. June 24, 2015. https://www.indexoncensorship.org/2015/06/poland-journalist-lukasz-masiak-fatally-beaten/. Accessed on January 12, 2016.
77. "Poland." Freedom House. 2015. https://freedomhouse.org/report/freedom-press/2015/poland. Accessed on January 12, 2016.
78. "Media Regulations: Normative Media Theory." University of Leicester. 2015. http://www.le.ac.uk/oerresources/media/ms7501/mod2unit11/page_07.htm. Accessed on January 11, 2016.
79. Taylor, Adam. "Poland's Controversial New Media Law Could Get It Booted off Eurovision." *Washington Post*, January 13, 2016, Worldviews sec. https://www.washingtonpost.com/news/worldviews/wp/2016/01/12/how-polands-controversial-new-media-law-could-effect-eurovision-europes-campy-song-contest/. Accessed on January 13, 2016.
80. "Concerns over New Law Intended to "transform" Poland's Public Media." IFex. December 15, 2015. https://www.ifex.org/poland/2015/12/15/media_reform/. Accessed on January 12, 2016.
81. Ibid.
82. Hombach, Jean-Pierre. *The Secret About Acta*. Hillsborough Street, North Carolina: Lulu Press, 2010, p. 407.
83. "Super Bomb: Why America's Enemies Fear The GBU-43/B Massive Ordnance Air Blast". 2017. *The National Interest*. http://nationalinterest.org/blog/the-buzz/super-bomb-why-americas-enemies-fear-the-gbu-43-b-massive-20171. Accessed on April 14, 2017.
84. Spoehr. 2017. "The 'Mother Of All Bombs' (MOAB) has been Dropped on Afghanistan. Here's What It Does (And Doesn't) Mean". Fox News. http://www.foxnews.com/opinion/2017/04/13/mother-all-bombs-moab-has-been-dropped-on-afghanistan-heres-what-it-does-and-doesnt-mean.html. Accessed on April, 17 2017.
85. "Washington's Weapon of Mass Destruction not Scaring Anybody". 2017. Sputniknews.Com. https://sputniknews.com/politics/201704141052655594-washington-weapon-mass-destruction-scare/. Accessed on April 14, 2017.
86. "US MOAB Strike Sends 'Important Message To Enemies' – Senator Graham". 2017. Sputniknews.Com. https://sputniknews.com/military/201704141052653206-moab-strike-message-graham/. Accessed on April 14, 2017.

87. "U.S. Drops Largest Non-Nuclear Bomb In Afghanistan - Xinhua | English.News.Cn." 2017. News.Xinhuanet.Com. http://news.xinhuanet.com/english/2017-04/14/c_136206842.htm. Accessed on April 15, 2017.
88. "New Arms Race Risk Increases As U.S. Drops Largest Non-Nuclear Bomb In Afghanistan: Russian Senator – Xinhua | English.News.Cn." 2017. News.Xinhuanet.Com. http://news.xinhuanet.com/english/2017-04/14/c_136209247.htm. Accessed on April 18, 2017.
89. "US Says 'Mother Of All Bombs' Hits ISIL In Afghanistan". 2017. Aljazeera.Com. http://www.aljazeera.com/news/2017/04/drops-mother-bombs-isil-afghanistan-170413174730383.html. Accessed on April 18, 2017.
90. Ibid.
91. "Mixed Reaction In Afghanistan Over Nangarhar Bombing". 2017. Aljazeera.Com. http://www.aljazeera.com/video/news/2017/04/mixed-reaction-afghanistan-nangarhar-bombing-170414143849115.html. Accessed on April 18, 2017.
92. "MOAB Attack: Condemnation, Praise Over Massive Bombing". 2017. Aljazeera.Com. http://www.aljazeera.com/news/2017/04/hamid-karzai-condemns-mother-bombs-170414124459611.html. Accessed on April 18, 2017.
93. n. 10.
94. "36 ISIS Affiliates Killed By US MOAB Attack". 2017. Bakhtarnews.Com.Af. http://www.bakhtarnews.com.af/eng/security/item/28272-36-isis-affiliates-killed-by-us-moab-attack.html. Accessed on April 17, 2017.
95. "IS' Amaq News Agency Publishes Infographic Downplaying MOAB'S Impact". 2017. News.Siteintelgroup.Com. https://news.siteintelgroup.com/Jihadist-News/is-amaq-news-agency-publishes-infographic-downplaying-moab-s-impact.html. Accessed on April 18, 2017.
96. n. 13.
97. "Pence Warns N. Korea 'Era Of Strategic Patience Is Over'". 2017. Kyodo News+. https://english.kyodonews.net/news/2017/04/92b6f541bd3c-update3-pence-warns-n-korea-era-of-strategic-patience-is-over.html?phrase=Afghanistan&words=Afghanistan. Accessed on April 18, 2017.
98. The search result for MOAB yielded nil result in Kyodonews website.
99. https://twitter.com/DavidCornDC/status/665310534669996032?lang=en
100. https://twitter.com/realdonaldtrump/status/552955075715690496
101. https://twitter.com/RepJeffDuncan?ref_src=twsrc%5Etfw
102. http://www.theguardian.com/commentisfree/2015/jun/03/us-isis-syria-iraq